Drinking from the Sacred Well

Also by John Matthews

The Winter Solstice
The Bardic Source Book
The Druid Source Book
Healing the Wounded King
The Mystic Grail
Sources of the Grail
The Celtic Shaman
Paths to Peace
The Grail: Quest for Eternal Life

Drinking from the Sacred Well

Personal Voyages of Discovery with the Celtic Saints

John Matthews

Go dtuga Dia deoch duit as an tobar nach dtrann.
May God give you to drink from the well that never runs dry.
—*Traditional Irish prayer*

HarperSanFrancisco
A Division of HarperCollinsPublishers

FIRST EDITION
Designed by Joseph Rutt

Library of Congress Cataloging-in-Publication Data
Matthews, John
    Drinking from the sacred well : personal voyages of discovery with the Celtic saints / John Matthews.—1st ed.
    Includes bibliographical references.
    ISBN 0-06-251561-6 (Cloth)
    ISBN 0-06-251562-4 (pbk.)
    1. Christian saints, Celtic—Biography. I. Title.
BR754.AIM36 1998
270'.092'3916—dc21   98–30395

98 99 00 01 02 ❖/RRD 10 9 8 7 6 5 4 3 2 1

To Ari Berk for the germ of the idea,
and to all who journey

Contents

Acknowledgments

I am indebted to the many scholars of Celtic tradition who have gone before, especially Kuno Meyer and Charles Plummer, whose translations of the lives of the saints provided much of the material from which this book was crafted. A deep debt also to my wife, Caitlín, for her peerless work as a translator, and for allowing me to reproduce some of her work here, especially on the Augury of Brighid.

Calendar of
the Celtic Saints in This Book

Kentigern	January 14
Maedoc	January 31
Brighid	February 2
Berach	February 15
David	March 1
Senan	March 8
Patrick	March 17
Brendan	May 16
Kevin	June 3
Columba	June 9
Mochuda	August 19
Ciaran	September 9

Ímmrama: Voyages of the Soul

Look you out
northeastwards
over the mighty ocean,
teeming with sea-life;
home of seals,
sporting, splendid,
its tide has discovered fullness.

—*J. M., after James Carney*

The theme of this book is voyaging. Voyages of the soul, voyages of the heart, voyages of the mind. Voyages through the world and beyond the world. Voyages into light, drawn from the lives of the Celtic saints, those remarkable men and women who sought to better understand the world in which they lived, first by turning inward and considering the soul's journey, then by turning outward to study the movement of the tides and the circling of the stars, finding there the natural rhythms of life and death reflected.

We are all engaged on such a journey, however we choose to interpret it. It may be the journey from birth to death, from morning to evening, from war to peace; or it may be the journey that is our search for meaning, truth, or validity. It is this journey that permeates our whole life, and that often promotes within us a sense of longing, whether for the place we came from or the place to which we are headed.

Along the way we will meet some who possess the certainty of their goal, their destination, and others who express their passage through life in a wandering fashion, seemingly as directionless as the others are purposeful. We ourselves may fall into either category, or sometimes into both. There will be periods during which we feel confident, directed in our journey. At other times we may feel a boundless sense of loss and bewilderment, when the journey seems pointless, directionless, static. It is at times such as these that we turn to others for direction, and if we are fortunate, find it in the person and presence of a friend whose journey is at a different stage, who has passed through the point where we find ourselves, who knows the treacherous shoals or violent undercurrents of the sea on which we are both embarked.

It is just such fellow journeyers as these that constitute the subjects of this book. They are the saints of the Celtic people, men and women who saw divinity in everything and who undertook the journey with a sense of purpose. Natural wisdom was their cauldron, and they drew deep drafts from it. They sought to express the purpose and purity of all life in their own journeys. They had two names for themselves: *Celli Dé*, "the children of God," and *peregrini*, "voyagers," terms that admirably describe the twin poles of their lives—their belief in the family of the created universe, and their desire to traverse its every part, whether in the spirit or in the flesh.

The names of more than ten thousand Celtic saints have survived, some of them recorded only in the land, as place-names that summon up long-forgotten events, legends, and miracles that have vanished, along with their owners, back into the mists from which they came. Aidan, Columba, and Ninian; Brighid, Ciaran, and Kevin; Samthan, Maedoc, and David—their names form a litany, memorials of a past that is long since gone, but that in our own time has acquired an urgent energy.

The stories of these people have something to tell us: something both about ourselves—about our own soul's journey—and about the environment in which we live. They can help us mend some of the broken fragments of the past and the present. From the loam of their examples comes a new growth, a rich heritage upon which we can draw. Their journeys tell us about our own world, about the spiritual voyage on which we have already embarked. Their voices come to us strongly, echoing down the years, relaying their passionate regard for nature, their sense of timelessness, their knowledge of other worlds.

A whole genre of stories—*immrama*, literally, "rowings about"—treats of these voyages, outlining them in images as clear as the water that bubbles out of the ground at a hundred sacred wellheads scattered throughout the Celtic landscape. Through these we can follow the adventures of Saint Brendan "the Navigator," who sought a secret country where he could be closer to God, and whose voyage took him to a series of islands representing stages of the soul's journey.

Not all the Celtic saints found their way by water. Others loved the land as much or more. Their journeys, to still different states of being, took their qualities from animal, bird, or fish. Saint Kevin of Glendalough was taught by a blackbird, and was followed and helped by animals throughout his life. Saint Brighid of Kildare, who grew to share the attributes of an ancient Celtic goddess, was the daughter of a milkmaid and took as her symbol the cow whose milk reflected her role as foster mother to Christ. Others took upon them the very nature of the creatures who befriended them: Columba was called "the crane cleric" because of his wisdom; Saint Ninian was referred to as "like a bee [who] formed for himself the honeycombs of wisdom." Patrick expressed his deepest feeling for the natural world in the form of a work that he called "the Deer's Cry." These were not accidental images—the Celtic saints understood the value of keeping in touch with creation through its nonhuman representatives.

Their world was a strange and wonderful place, where fire could be carried in the bare hands without fear of burning, spirits and angels conferred with, wild animals tamed with a word. But the most wonderful and profound mystery that the Celts have to teach us is about our uniquely intimate relationship with the natural world. We are wonderful beings—beings of light—and we inhabit a remarkable universe, although nowadays we seldom recognize this. By cutting ourselves off from nature, by telling ourselves that we are separate, unique, powerful in our own right, we are doing the equivalent of cutting off our limbs. None of us would call ourselves whole without hands or feet; yet we repeatedly sever our contact with the rest of creation, shutting ourselves up in overheated rooms with the TV and the artificiality of a world created in our own image.

The Celts were the opposite of this. They followed a path of total involvement with the world about them—not only in the physical world, but through their spirituality, which was itself an outward expression of inner things. Through identifying with the natural world they were able to place their personal experiences in context. We can do the same. The highly sensitized covering of the soul, which can react so strongly when it feels slighted or attacked in any way, reaches a new point of strength when it is no longer placed at the center of everything. Shifting the center to another place, we become new beings and are able to recognize our own inner journey in the context of a larger whole.

The same is true of the Celtic saints whose stories you are about to read, just as it is true of the Druids who went before them. The shift from "pagan" to "Christian" was for the Celts the smallest of steps; it involved no wrenching of the soul from the extreme of one path to the extreme of another. For almost eight hundred years, from the fifth to the twelfth century, the Celtic church did much to keep alive the traditions of the native people, while at the same time promoting the idea of Classical learning. The same love of the land, the same honoring of the spirit, the same dance of life, continued unabated despite the change from many gods to one. The essence of the Celtic deities, who were an inevitable expression of the natural world and the holiness of everything, flowed into the container of the new spirituality and changed it from within. Patterns of the inner life, or the place of the human spirit within the universe as a whole, continued as they always had. It was as if two rivers, one flowing out of the east, the other from the west, met and combined and became an even greater confluence.

When we read, therefore, in the lives of the Celtic saints, we perceive the same fundamental truths that are present in the lives of the gods and heroes of the past: a love of the earth, of the pattern of the seasons, of the magical presence of the animals, of the beauty of the revealed world.

It is this that has given rise to a belief in the existence of a "Celtic church." In a sense, there never was any such thing— at least not as a separate entity with its own governing body or fixed rule. The eternal verities remained, whatever the outward changes, the petty squabbles over the dating of Easter and Christmas, and the shape of the monastic tonsure. The journey toward a world of numinous spirituality continued regardless of individual beliefs, the expression of a spiritual unity that gathered strands of wisdom from all over the Celtic world and made of them something like a whole. This spirituality, drawn from the peoples of Ireland, Scotland, Wales, Cornwall, Brittany, and the Isle of Man, possessed a commonality of imagery and belief that extended far beyond the bounds of Christian theology at the time. It was also, as a recent writer has put it,

> very much a child of the pagan culture which preceded it, one that valued poetic imagination and artistic creativity, kinship relations and the warmth of the hearth, the wonder of stories and the guidance of dreams. It was a spirituality profoundly affected by the beauty of the landscape, the powerful presence of the sea, and the swift passage at night of the full moon across open skies.
>
> —E. C. Sellner, *Wisdom of the Celtic Saints*

From this marriage came, in time, a high degree of learning and wisdom, which gave us the *Book of Kells*, the elaborate and beautiful high crosses that combined Christian and pagan ideas, and the idea of the hospitality of the heart, which enabled all kinds of people to meet and share their beliefs without fear. The men and women who taught the truths of the new God never completely lost touch with the old deities of wood and water and stone. They reached behind the identity of deity to the heart of matter itself—and in so doing left behind a legacy that speaks as clearly to us today as it did to the people of that long-ago time. This legacy takes the form of a series of messages: that we should acknowledge our place in the universe as a whole; that we should recognize the holiness in all of that creation, not just our own part of it; that we should undertake our journey in the knowledge that it is part of an ongoing process of completion. These messages are still embedded in the stories you are about to read, and they are as relevant as they ever were—indeed more so since we have cut ourselves off from the rest of creation.

From the meeting of pagan and Christian came a spirituality that combined elements from both approaches to life, death, and the Otherworld. While the Celtic monks never really strayed from the course of their beliefs, the color of that belief was subtly changed. Elements of the older faith entered their lives, giving a subtle turn to the stories in which they were framed. Thus, while we hear much of Saint Patrick's attacks on paganism in Ireland, we do not often hear of his response to the enthusiastic followers who cut down a grove of sacred trees to clear land on which to build a church. Dismayed, Patrick ordered that the trees be left where they had fallen rather than used as building timbers, and that another site be chosen. He later said that he could conceive of no worse sound than that of an ax striking a tree in Ireland— scarcely the thoughts of someone determined to stamp out the country's older faith.

In the story of Saint Ciaran, who became famous for his relationship with representatives of the animal kingdom, we hear that on his first arrival in Ireland he was granted a vision of a vast tree growing from the center of the land, islanded by a mighty river. Ciaran's spiritual mentor told him that it was a symbol of the enduring quality of his mission, but Ciaran saw it as something deeper. He was moved to found a monastery near a river in the center of Ireland, and Clonmacnoise became one of the most important foundations in the Western world, famed for the learning and wisdom of its monks.

In its five hundred years of semiautonomy the Celtic church promoted the value of women, whom it allowed to celebrate the mysteries openly and equally (much to the dismay of its Roman brethren); it honored the created world as a place of vibrant life and goodness, addressing God as "Lord of the Elements" and angels as "Shining Ones"; and it made the animal kingdom an important expression of its spirituality. As an anonymous ninth-century poem has it:

> To go to Rome—
> Is little profit, endless pain;
> The Master that you seek in Rome
> You find at home, or seek in vain.
> —*Trans. Frank O'Connor*

These words could be said to stand as a testimony for the majority of the Celtic saints.

The work of these holy men and women who had been called by God can thus be seen to continue that of the visionaries and seers of an older world: seeking silence and solitariness as a means of opening the doors between the realms of flesh and spirit, and opening themselves to the natural world at an astonishingly deep level. Indeed, as one reads the lives of these ancient holy people, one cannot help seeing that there is a longing for the brighter colors of the past, and a reluctance to let go of the older traditions. The use of poetic and magical names for matters that had far more prosaic terminology in eastern doctrine forms a living record of the people who wrote down their beliefs for those who came after.

Much of this is summed up in a poem attributed to the seventh-century Irish saint Manchan, through which we catch a glimpse of the world in which the Celtic saints lived:

Manchan's Prayer

I wish, O Son of the living God,
O ancient eternal King,
For a hidden hut in the wilderness
To be my dwelling.

And, quite near,
A beautiful wood,
Nursing many-voiced birds,
Offering me shelter.

A warm southern aspect,
A little brook crossing the floor,
A choice land with generous gifts
To nurture every plant.

A few good men—
The number does not matter—
Humble men to pray
Daily to the King of Life.

A pleasant church
With a linen altar cloth,
A dwelling-place for God,
A candle to light the scriptures.

This is the husbandry I seek
The bounty I would wish for—
Hens, salmon, trout, and bees,
Food enough for all.

These gifts from the King of Heaven
I would pray for every day,
Seeking to be seen
In the place I had made.

—*J. M., after Kuno Meyer*

These simple requests—for food, a roof, and a quiet place in the woods—epitomize a generation of people who sought to preserve a way of life that was already passing, and to inspire those who came to listen to them with the wonder of creation. They taught that the natural world, and the creatures that inhabited it, was filled with a holy and ineffable light—that same light that drew them to travel to the ends of the earth and beyond into the Otherworld, in search of those visionary truths that all need but few think of seeking for themselves. Their lives are a triumphant expression of wholeness, or inner certainty, qualities that gave them the strength to see their own journeys—seldom easy or comfortable—through to the end.

If there are three essential aspects to the spirituality of the Celtic saints, they would have to be silence and contemplation, the love of nature, and the love of learning. This triad—a form beloved of the Celts—colors all the stories included here. From them we can learn a great deal about the nature of the spiritual heritage of the saints. We too can open nature's book, study the patterns of our lives in the silence of the soul's journey, and learn to value knowledge not just for its own sake, but for the way it shapes and forms us. Each story has been chosen to illustrate one aspect or another of the voyages on which we are all engaged, and at the end of each you will find brief Meditation Points, designed to lead on from the story you have just read and to help you connect more directly with it.

This is very much in keeping with the original texts from which these stories are drawn. The original "lives" were written as exemplars, teaching aids that were hardly ever true biographies as we would understand them today. The lives of these remarkable men and women were seen to hold up a mirror to people everywhere, and while today we may find ourselves hard-pressed to emulate them as might once have been the case, we can still learn from them. As spiritual biographies they project the story of the human soul, and the stories they tell—dramatic, moving, and inspiring by turns—offer a rich fare for the seeker today.

The stories that make up this book are intended to make you think, to ask questions about your inner and outer voyages. They are full of lore both rich and strange, deriving from a people whose imaginative powers have seldom if ever been equaled. Whether you step with Brendan onto the deck of a ship headed for a strange and wondrous country, or follow the wandering life of Ciaran, or enter the visionary world of Maedoc, you will find here echoes of your own journey, of the questions that arise in your life and that fuel your ongoing journey. You will also find, following each of the stories, a poem from the Celtic tradition that reflects the mystical relationship between the *Celli Dé* and the world about them. Many of these are newly translated, and I have tried to capture the innate beauty of these lines to the best of my ability.

The majority of the stories you will find here derive from ancient sources. It will be noticed that most of the stories are of Irish origin. This is simply because there is a far higher survival rate of the original documents that tell of the Irish saints. While there were an equally large number of British, Scottish, and Breton saints, in many cases their lives are fragmentary or in various ways unsuitable for a modern audience. The collections of Irish stories, such as those from the fourteenth-century *Book of Lismore,* or the later *Vita Sanctorum Hiberniae,* are rich and full of poetry.

Once one begins to look at the whole range of stories, the thing that strikes one about them is the wide variety of incidents they contain. While there are overlaps, episodes that turn up in more than one saint's life, there are far more that never repeat themselves. And the richness of the literary tradition is wonderful. Thus in one story we read how Senan battles with the Druids, while in the life of David of Wales there is a dark story of murder and sacrifice balanced by a wonderful tale of the saint's horse, which could gallop across the water as though it were on dry land.

In all the stories included here I have sought to find wonder, the expression of spiritual truth, and poetry. In the process, while never intentionally steering the content away from the original intent, I have tried to go beyond into a place where all spiritual paths meet and reflect one another. Thus, I have modified the sometimes extreme monasticism of the writers (who were, after all, monks themselves, as well as fine storytellers) and have chosen to retell those episodes that reflect a larger picture. In this way I hope to make the stories accessible to a wider audience, to set them free of the confines of theology. To this end I have allowed myself considerable freedom to reshape the original stories, while remaining faithful to the spirit and occasionally the words in which they were first recorded. This approach not only opens up the stories of the Celtic saints; it also shows how much their biographers were indebted to the pre-Christian storytellers whose works they clearly knew. These stories were always intended to teach by example, and in the current retelling I have tried to allow their innate spiritual messages to emerge into the light of day where they can be enjoyed by a modern audience.

These stories (often written by those who knew the saints personally) celebrate the voyages of the spirit that these remarkable men and women undertook. At a time when we are all in search of new truths, new ways of looking at old truths, they have much to teach us. They can become our soul-friends—*anam chara*—on our own journey; and read with an open heart—just as they were set down with an open heart—they offer a series of beacons to be followed and experienced for ourselves, whatever course our own journey may have taken. The realizations that follow release a tide of love within us: love for one another, for God, and for the world in which we live and move and have our being. As we acknowledge the power of the voyage, and of our own place within it, we awaken as if from a long sleep. The blood courses in our veins with renewed vigor and we turn again to the tasks of daily living with new strength and purpose.

John Matthews
Oxford, 1998

In Search of
a Secret Country
Brendan of Clonfert

⊠ ⊠ ⊠

Seven years in all were they
On the voyage—fair was the band—
Seeking the Land of Promise
With its flocks, a strong subtle turn.

And they found it at last
In the high meeds of the ocean,
An island rich, everlasting, undivided,
Abounding in salmon, fair and beauteous.

—*Navigatio Brendani*

*With the story of Brendan we are plunged into a world where the
Voyage leads out of this world, out of ordinary, everyday
consciousness, into another place. The Land of Promise it is called
here, a name also applied to the Otherworld by pre-Christian Celts.
It is the first sign that we are entering a place where two ways meet;
the old magic of the Time Before and the new magic of Palestine are
joining hands. When Brendan sees an angel who instructs him to*

set forth on a voyage of inner discovery he stands in the shoes of older heroes, like Bran mac Ferbal, who undertook an earlier voyage after a faery woman came to draw him away. In both cases the purpose is the same; angel and faery each comes to offer an opportunity to discover something new and wonderful. Indeed, the parallels between the Christian "Voyage of Brendan" and the pagan "Voyage of Bran" are so close as to include the names of certain islands and virtually identical adventures taking place on them. From this we can see that the later storytellers not only knew the older tales but were influenced by them when it came to the description of the otherworldly islands visited by Brendan.

Brendan lived from about A.D. 486 to 578. In that time Christianity had been established in Ireland for some time (Saint Patrick—389–461—was its main source) so that Brendan was part of a tradition that had taken hold and was putting down deep roots. Born at Annagh on the Bay of Tralee, he became a monk and later an abbot and founded monasteries at Clonfert and Ardfert. He traveled widely, including to Iona, where he met with Columba, as well as to Wales, Britain, and Gaul.

There are more than one hundred manuscript versions of the Voyage of Brendan, many of them differing markedly and adding other islands. I have worked primarily from the version ascribed to a "poor friar" named Michael O'Clery and dated 1629. Although late, this version seems to me to capture the wonder and innocence of the story, which so clearly harks back to the adventurers of earlier voyagers in the Celtic tradition.

THE BIRTH OF BRENDAN

The day Brendan was born the whole sky above his village of Alltraighe Caille lit up with fire. The wise bishop Erc said that a great soul had come into the world that night. Brendan was the son of Findlug who, the night before his birth, dreamed that her breast became golden, as though filled with light. When he heard this, Bishop Erc said that the child was to have a special destiny, and when he was one year old placed him in the care of a woman named Ita. Wise and full of wit, she cared for the child until he was five, at which time the bishop himself took him in and taught him the ways of Christ. Thus Brendan grew in stature and knowledge until he was a young man, when he saw an angel standing in a field of corn. The angel pointed westward, and though he did not understand it then, Brendan ever after wished to the west.

BARINTHUS'S STORY

One day when Brendan was at a place called Leim na Subaltaige a man named Barinthus came to see him. Now this Barinthus was known to possess a great knowledge of the tides and the stars, and was a great sailor. He told Brendan a story and this was the way of it.

Barinthus had a son named Mernoc who, when he came of age, decided to leave home in search of adventure. He was gone a long while before his father received news of him. He had, it seemed, found his way to an island where there were a number of *peregrini,* holy men who sought to learn the ways of God more deeply through wandering and living in isolation. Desiring to know more, Barinthus set sail and in three days arrived at the island. The *peregrini* came out of their huts like a swarm of bees, clustering around the visitors as though there were pure honey. Barinthus spent some time with Mernoc and his brethren, learning their ways. They lived simply on the island, eating only apples and nuts, studying the paths of the stars and the movement of the tides, which sang to them day and night.

Then Mernoc came to his father and led him to the shore where a little boat lay at rest. "Father," he said, "let us get into the boat. It will take us to a place that is called the Land of the Saints, where there are many wonders."

Together they stepped into the boat, which at once drew away from the shore, though no one could see how it was driven or who steered it. A mist settled over the water, so that neither Barinthus nor Mernoc could see where they were headed, until suddenly there was a great light ahead, and the mist began to clear. They found themselves close to the shore of a new land, where white sands edged the water, and the trees that grew there were heavy with fruit.

Father and son went ashore on this beautiful country and for the next fifteen days they wandered without seeing anyone. Then they came to a wide river that blocked their path. On the far bank they could see a place that seemed to them even more wonderful than that in which they stood, but there was no way to cross the river, which ran swift and high between its banks.

As they stood, there came in sight a man who was clad in garments of radiant light. He approached them directly and addressed them by their names. "Beloved friends," he said, "you may not pass beyond the river. Thus much has been revealed to you so that you may know of its existence and tell everyone you meet of its beauty. For this is the Land of Promise and the Land of the Saints."

Then they asked the man whence he came and what his name might be. And he answered them thus: "Why do you ask me this? You would be better employed asking about this place. Though you do not realize it, a year has passed since you stepped ashore. In all that time you have never seen the sun set or wanted for food and drink. This might be the lot of all if only they remembered this place. For all have been here, and yet they have lost the way back to it."

Barinthus and his son were saddened by this, and turned away. They returned to the boat and the man accompanied them all the way, talking to them of the ways of the world and the ways of the spirit and how these might be brought together. But when they were arrived at the shore he vanished away they knew not how or where. Then they climbed into the boat, which drew away from the shore and sped back across the mist-draped water to the island where Mernoc lived.

The holy men came to meet them and inquired of their journey. Barinthus and his son told them everything that had occurred and said, "You are fortunate indeed, for you live close to the Land of Promise." Then Barinthus took leave of his son and set forth wandering through the world, so that he might tell everyone he met about the wonderful land.

THE VOYAGE BEGINS

When he had heard this story Brendan could not rest until he had visited the Land of Promise for himself. For now he understood the meaning of the angel that had pointed to the west. And that night, as he slept, he saw the angel again, and it said to him: "Arise, Brendan. That which you have longed for shall be yours." And the angel told him to choose companions and prepare a ship in which to begin a great voyage.

When he awoke Brendan did as the angel had bidden. He gathered about him fourteen other men from Leim na Subaltaige and told them that he desired to set forth in search of the wonderful land. And he told them also of the angel's words, and when they heard this they declared that they wished to go more than anything else in the world.

So Brendan and his companions went to a place that ever after was known as Suide Brenainn (Brendan's Seat), from where they looked out upon the ocean. For Brendan knew that it was from here that they would set forth. So they set about preparing a small craft and provisioning it for several weeks at sea—for though they had no idea of the distance they must sail, Brendan's inner voice told him that they would find further sustenance when they needed it.

When all was prepared, the company embarked; but just as they were about to set sail, a man clad like a Fool came hurrying up and begged to be allowed to go with them. And, since there was one last place on the ship, Brendan gave it to him.

Then they set sail forthwith to the west.

The Island of Hospitality

For days they sailed toward the Summer Solstice. The wind blew strongly and they had no need of navigation. But after fifteen days the wind dropped and they were forced to row onward. After a time they grew weary and looked to Brendan for advice. He said, "Do not fear. God's angel is steering us. Ship all the oars and the rudder but leave the sail set. If we give ourselves up to the will of the sea, we shall come to no harm."

They did as Brendan told them, and for the next forty days the craft was driven by fitful winds and wild water. Soon all their food and most of their water was gone. Then they espied an island. To their dismay it was a high and rocky place with no sign of a safe harbor.

To add to their discomfort they could see several places where freshwater streams fell over the edge of the cliffs and down to the sea. At first they tried to sail close to the cliffs and to lean out over the side with drinking vessels in which to catch some of the water. But when he saw this, Brendan ordered them to stop. "We must trust to God's angel to guide us to the right place. In three days we shall find a landing place. Until then we must bide out time."

Sure enough, on the third day they found an opening in the cliffs, and though it was very sheer and narrow they managed to steer a course within, and found themselves in a sheltered bay. There they disembarked, and there, as they stood upon the land, a dog came and laid its head on Brendan's feet.

"Is this not a good messenger?" said Brendan. "Let us follow it."

In a short time they arrived at the gates of a town, which were open in welcome. Yet there was not a single person to be seen, and they grew afraid at this. But Brendan encouraged them to enter, and in a short while they saw before them a great hall, with its doors standing open, and inside they found tables laid with bread and wine and fish for all.

Brendan said, "Let us eat, for this feast is sent to reward our endeavor. And afterward you will find beds made ready for you."

So they ate hungrily, and never had food tasted better. Then they retired to rest.

For three days and three nights they rested and were served with such hospitality as they had never known, all without sight of those who served them. Then on the fourth day Brendan declared that they must set forth again. "Be careful," he said to them, "that no one takes anything from this island—not even water or bread."

And, because of the faith they had in Brendan, they set sail again from the island without taking any provisions. But before they had gone far the sails fell limp and the sea was becalmed. Brendan called to him all who were on the ship. "One of you has taken something from the island. We can go no farther until it is given back."

The man dressed like a Fool who had come late to the voyage fell at Brendan's feet and drew from within the bosom of his clothing a bridle inlaid with silver. He flung it down and burst out weeping.

"Let us return to the island," said Brendan.

At once the sails filled and the boat returned by way of the narrow channel to the inlet. There Brendan commanded the one who had stolen the bridle to go ashore and to return it whence it came.

As they were returning to the ship a youth came toward them along the shore, carrying a basket of bread and a flask of water. "I bring this gift to you, Brendan, with the thanks and blessings of your hosts. You still have far to go on your journey, but neither bread nor water will you lack until you are at your journey's end."

And with this the company returned to their craft and their voyage continued, and no matter how much they ate or drank of the bread and water, they never lacked for either until they arrived at their next landfall.

THE ÎSLAΠD OF BÎRDS

A few days after this they sighted another island. Low-lying and supporting neither grass nor sand, it seemed an inhospitable place. But the companions were glad to go ashore even in that barren spot and at once set about lighting a cooking fire. Brendan, however, stood on the deck of the ship and watched them with a smile, for his angel had told him the true nature of the island.

In a while as the fire grew hotter the whole island began to shake and shiver as if it were about to sink beneath the waves. The companions grew fearful and hastened back to the boat, where Brendan helped them aboard quickly. Then they pulled up their anchor and watched as the island began to move away from them of its own accord! The companions turned to Brendan for understanding and he laughed aloud. "Do you not know the nature of this island?" he asked. They shook their heads. "It is no island at all," said Brendan, "but a great fish—the greatest that ever sailed the seas. God's angel has told me that its name is Jasconius and that it sails forever in search of a mate."

The companions marveled greatly at this, and watched as their fire vanished into the dusk of the day, carried on the back of the great creature. Then many gave thanks for the wonders that filled the world, and they sailed on, looking always for the next landfall, which might be the gateway to the Land of Promise.

Soon they sighted another island and drawing up to its shore dropped anchor. It was a fair-seeming place, where the grass was starred with flowers in profusion and a grove of trees clustered on the horizon. Brendan led his companions ashore and they found a stream of very pure water from which they gratefully drank. Then they followed the course of the stream inland until they reached its source. There a most beautiful tree grew down over the water. Its height and size were remarkable in themselves, but the most astonishing thing about the tree was that it was covered with white birds. So thickly did they cluster on its branches that one could scarcely see its leaves.

Gazing upon this sight Brendan's eyes filled with tears and he wept aloud, calling upon God's angel to tell him the meaning of this wonder. As he did so, one of the birds flew down and settled beside them. The motion of its wings made a sound like the pealing of tiny bells.

Brendan looked at the bird and said, "If you are a messenger, speak and tell me why so many of your kind are gathered here."

At once the bird replied: "We are survivors of an ancient battle between the angels of light and dark. Because we took sides with neither one nor the other we must remain in the world, able to travel only in spirit form. Only on holy days are we permitted to take on the shape that you see. For today is Easter and you have been upon your voyage for a year. Six more years lie before you, but in the end you shall find the Land of Promise."

The companions listened in astonishment to this, for to them it seemed as though only a few weeks had passed. But Brendan smiled and gave thanks to the bird for its wisdom and watched as it rejoined its fellows. Then the whole company set about preparing to celebrate the holy festival, setting up a makeshift altar on a flat stone in the shadow of the great tree.

When the time came to sing praises to God for the wonder of creation and the blessing of Christ, the companions gathered about the foot of the tree, and there the birds who sat upon the branches like blossoms began to sing, and it seemed to them all that their voices formed words and that they sang as sweetly as a heavenly choir of angels.

And when they had finished celebrating they prepared to continue their journey. But as they were about to raise the anchor one of the white birds came again and settled upon the prow of the boat. Once again Brendan said that if this was God's messenger it should speak, and once again the bird obeyed. "In a year's time you shall return here and celebrate Easter just as you did this day, and you shall meet again with the great creature Jasconius. Sail on now, Brendan, and in time you shall find yourself on an island where only the wisest elders are to be found. There you shall celebrate Christmas."

Having delivered itself of these words the bird flew back to its place. As the ship drew away from the island shore they all heard voices raised once again in sacred song.

The Island of Ageless Elders

Now the ship carrying Brendan and his companions sailed for several weeks without sight of land. At the end of this time they saw a new island rising from the sea. But though they made directly for it they could not, at first, find anywhere to land. For another five days they sailed about, and it was only as they began to wonder whether they might ever find a harbor on this island that there appeared an entrance between high rocks. There they put in to the shore and stepping out of the boat found two wells sited close to each other. One gave forth water of such purity that it seemed to shine with its own light; the other was muddy and dark.

At first the companions would have rushed forward to drink, but Brendan stopped them. "I believe we are not meant to drink from either of these wells until we are give permission by those who live upon this isle."

As he spoke there came toward them a man of great age and gravity. He bowed to them in silence and beckoned them to follow. They made their way through a grove of trees and there before them was an enclosure with walls of stone. Within it were a number of round huts, clustered around a larger building in the center.

"What is this place?" asked Brendan. "Who lives here?"

The elder did not answer, but beckoned them to enter the enclosure. Brendan and his companions looked about and saw a number of men coming from the huts and making their way to the larger building, which they now saw was a church built of timbers and roofed in straw that shone as though made of gold.

Still in silence the companions were conducted into a refractory where tables were laid with loaves of extraordinary whiteness. As soon as they were seated a man came forward with a jug of water and served them all. Only now did the elder speak: "Welcome, voyagers to the Land of Promise! Drink deeply of this water that will enrich you, and eat of the food we have provided. But do not speak until all have eaten and we have celebrated the bounty of God together."

Thus in silence the travelers and their hosts ate and drank. Never had bread and water tasted so sweet. And when they were done the elder led them to the church. In its cool interior Brendan and his companions looked around and saw that the building was square and had two altars, each one made of crystal, with vessels of the same wondrous material. Twenty-four seats were set out in a circle around the church, and here the companions were given places.

All was done in strict silence, and they noticed that if any one of the island community wished to convey something to the elder he went and knelt before the venerable man and spoke not with words but with glances. The elder would listen with his inner senses and write whatever revelation he received on a wax tablet, which he then gave to the one who sought an answer.

Only when silent prayers had been offered up, and the mysteries celebrated with the vessels of crystal, did the elder finally give permission to speak. To Brendan and his companions he said: "I know you have many questions. Let me answer some of them even though you have not given them voice. We are a community who have lived together here on this island for more than eighty years. In that time none of us has grown any older or suffered a day of sickness. Every day we are brought sufficient loaves and roots to eat, though we have no idea whence they come. You have seen our two wells. They are a wonder, for one gives the purest water that we ever saw, and the other is constantly warm, so that we may wash ourselves daily and are always cleansed and refreshed. Thus we live here in silence for the most part, listening only to the inner voice of God that speaks to us every day, and that conveys to us the wisdom and spiritual goodness for which all yearn."

"Father," said Brendan, "may we stay here with you? Surely I know of no more wonderful place, unless it is the Land of Promise itself."

"You may not," replied the elder gently. "Nor should you need to ask this, for your road leads elsewhere. I tell you that soon you shall come to another place, the Island of the Three Choirs, and there one of your number will remain, but for the rest you shall journey onward, as it is given you to do."

While they spoke thus, darkness began to fall, but as the shadows lengthened within the church, a fiery arrow entered through a window and sped through the room, lighting all the lamps that hung before the two crystal altars. Then it flew out again and vanished none might say where.

"What does this mean?" asked Brendan.

"It is one of the mysteries of this place," replied the elder. "Observe how the light can be seen burning in the center of each bowl. Yet I tell you that it is never consumed. In the morning the light will flicker out, and tomorrow it will be lit again just as you saw it now. In all our time here we have never had to replenish it once. Truly it is a spiritual light."

That night Brendan and the elder kept vigil together, and in the morning the voyagers were invited to remain on the island until Epiphany, and to celebrate the feast of Christmas there, just as had been foretold.

THE ISLAND OF THE WELL OF SLEEP

When the feast days were over, Brendan and his companions prepared to depart. They provisioned their boat and received the blessing of the ageless elders before raising anchor and setting forth again. Winds and tides took them, and they sailed on for many days before they sighted land again. This time the island where they landed seemed hospitable.

The companions were eager to go ashore and replenish their stocks of food and water, and when they had disembarked they found a well of clear water close to the shore. Around it grew plants of many kinds, many of them edible, while in a stream that ran nearby they found plentiful fish.

Brendan told them to gather as much food as they wished but to be careful about how much water they drank. "For," said he, "it has been made plain to me that we should drink only sparingly of this spring."

Some of the companions chose to interpret this as taking no more than one cup; others thought they should have two; others, three. Those who took the most fell asleep almost at once and remained unconscious for three days. Those who took two cups slept for two days. Those who took only one slept for a day and a night and awoke refreshed.

"It seems to me that we should leave this place," said Brendan. And when they had replenished their stocks of food and water, they departed hurriedly, sailing north, though they knew not where they were bound.

The Island of Birds Again

Their course took them again to the Island of Birds, and just as had been foretold they celebrated Easter there once again. And before that they found themselves crossing the path of Jasconius, the great creature of the sea on whose back they had camped a year before. But always Brendan drove them onward, longing ever more deeply to see the Land of Promise.

One day when they were far from land they sighted a huge and terrible beast in the distance which, when it saw them, turned in their direction. The companions cried out in fear and began to pray aloud to God. But Brendan rebuked them for their lack of faith and commanded them to look again. When they did so, they saw another monster, which breathed both fire and smoke, rise from the water between them and the advancing creature. Then they watched a great battle between the two, and when it was over there were only pieces of the first monster floating in the sea.

Soon after that, they saw the shore of a large island covered with trees, and there they landed, glad of the chance to rest and refresh themselves. There, floating in the water of the bay where they had landed, they saw a part of the great beast that they had feared would kill them. Brendan ordered them to drag it ashore and to light a fire and cook it. "For," he said, "that which would have eaten of our flesh, we shall eat instead."

That night they dined well, for the flesh of the beast was particularly sweet. And next morning they set forth again.

The Island of the Three Choirs

Soon after this they espied a new island, very flat and treeless. Brendan looked toward it with his inner sight and said: "On that island are three choirs, just as we were told by the Ageless Elder. One consists of boys, one of youths, and a third of elders. One of us will not return from there."

The companions looked at one another in wonder, for they knew that Brendan was seldom mistaken in his visioning. For as time passed he was increasingly aware of how things must be, and of the meaning of events that took place on the voyage.

Soon they came to the shore and disembarked. The island was so flat and bare that they saw the three choirs at once. The boys were clad in white robes, the youths in blue, and the elders in purple. All three choirs went about constantly, moving from place to place on the island; only when they sang did they remain still. And, since one or the other was constantly singing and giving forth praises, the choirs were in perpetual motion, following some rhythm of heart or soul that neither Brendan nor his fellows could perceive. Yet their song was more wondrous and moving than anything they had ever heard.

As the day advanced a cloud of extraordinary brightness settled over the island, so that they could only hear the voices of the choirs but see nothing of them. Thus night fell and the voyagers slept to the sound of singing. And in the morning they awoke to the same bright song. Then one of the leaders of the choirs came forward with a basket of purple fruit and laid it in the boat. "Now give to us that one among you who has the finest voice, for one of our number has but lately died and another is needed."

Brendan turned to the man dressed like a Fool, who had been the last to join the company, and who had stolen the silver bridle. The man stepped forward with tears in his eyes. "I have long known that this would be my path," he said, "and the song calls out to me."

Then they set sail again, and were soon far from the island. Yet still they could hear the songs of the three choirs and marveled greatly at the beauty of their singing. Then they feasted on the purple fruit, which tasted like the finest honey and gave enough juice to feed them all.

The İsland of the Crystal Pillar

And so they sailed on for many more days, until they came to a place where the sea was so clear that they could see right to the bottom, and there were numerous hosts of fish swimming in such a way that it seemed to the companions that they followed a pattern. Some were afraid because of this and called to the others to keep silent lest they attract the attention of these strange fish. But Brendan told them to put aside their fear, and he began to sing aloud, encouraging his companions to do the same. Soon they were all singing together, and as they did so the fish began to rise to the surface until they surrounded the boat in their thousands.

There they stayed for many hours, always keeping the same distance between themselves and the boat, flowing around the craft in wide arcs, flashing fins and tails at the voyagers as though in silent salute. Then, just as suddenly, they were gone, and the sea was still.

Next morning the companions espied a pillar rising from the sea. At first it seemed close, but as day followed day and it seemed no nearer, they began to see how vast it was. Four days later they were close enough to see that the pillar stretched so far up into the heavens it seemed to touch the sky itself. Hanging from the pillar was a great net, the meshes of which were so wide that four men could have walked through them without touching. The company were greatly desirous of passing within the net, so that they might examine the nature of the pillar, yet the net was too small to allow the ship to go through. Therefore Brendan ordered his companions to ship their oars and to unstep the mast. When this was done they were able to steer between the meshes of the great web and so found themselves close to the pillar.

None could be certain from what substance it was made, though it seemed like crystal. As they sailed around it they saw that it had four sides, and that each one was carved with intricate patterns, and that here and there windows and ledges were cut into the sides. Some spoke of climbing it, but that Brendan forbade, for his angel told him it was not appropriate for them to do so.

That night they anchored close to the pillar, and for several hours after the sun had set they could still feel the heat coming from the pillar. In the morning they sailed on and found themselves on another side of the pillar. There, set in one of the carved niches, they found a crystal chalice, and at

Brendan's bidding they took it aboard and used it to celebrate the mystery of the Eucharist.

Then they set forth again, passing once more through the meshes of the giant net. Setting the sail and unshipping the oars, they proceeded once again toward the north—for in this direction it now seemed to Brendan they must continue until they reached their goal.

THE ISLAND OF SMITHS

Not long after this they saw a dark and craggy island on the horizon. Smoke arose from it as though from a hundred fires, and it was bare of either trees or grass.

Brendan frowned. "I do not like this place," he said. "Yet the wind is driving us closer to it."

As he spoke they came within clear sight of the island and saw that it seemed the most desolate place they had ever known. Huge piles of slag lay about everywhere, and there were signs that mining and smelting had taken place there for long ages. As the boat drifted nearer they saw that the island was covered in forges, from which huge distorted plumes of smoke arose, darkening the sky. As they looked, one of the smiths came out and stared at them. He was huge and hairy, with skin darkened by his work. When he saw the voyagers he let out a great roar and disappeared into his forge, emerging moments after with a red-hot boulder, which he flung high into the air. It passed very close to the boat and fell into the sea, which at once began to boil and bubble.

Brendan ordered the oars to be run out and they drew swiftly away from the island. More of the shaggy smiths came in sight, all carrying hot stones that they flung toward the ship. It seemed as though the whole island were ablaze with one great fire, and the sea on all sides boiled like a cooking pot. But despite being in mortal fear the companions rowed steadily, and gradually the island of smiths fell away behind them, until it was only a red stain on the water.

The Island of the Hermit

The next island they came upon was small and desolate. It was hard indeed to find a place to land, and when they had finally done so Brendan commanded them all to remain on the boat until he had sought permission from the island's inhabitants for them to come ashore.

Walking inland he came to a cliff where the mouth of a cave gaped in the rock. In front of it a small spring bubbled forth and in front of the spring sat a man whose white hair grew so plentifully that it completely covered him. Other than this he was naked, and Brendan marveled at his fortitude and his serenity.

When he saw Brendan approaching the aged man rose to his feet and gave a warm greeting, inviting Brendan to bring his companions ashore. He greeted them all by name, astonishing them with the power of his inner sight. Brendan praised him and asked him to speak to them of his life.

"My name is Paul," said the old hermit. "Once I was a monk whose task was to look after the burial place of all the brothers. One day I was preparing a new plot for one who was expected to die soon, when there came to me a stranger who commanded me to dig another grave. When I asked his name he told me that he was the father of my own monastery, no less than the blessed Patrick himself. He told me that he had died the day before, and that soon they would bring his body to be buried there. Then he swore me to silence and told me to go to the shore, where I would find a boat waiting to take me to the place I needed to be.

"In the morning I did just as the blessed Patrick told me, and there sure enough was a little boat with a single sail awaiting me. As I stepped in, the sail filled and it bore me across the ocean to this island. Once I stepped ashore the boat turned about of its own accord and returned the way it had come. Since then I have lived here alone save for a wonderful creature, an otter, who brings me a fish in its mouth every day, and has done so for the last thirty years. I live simply in this cave, and drink from the pure water of the spring that you see. God takes care of all my needs. I am ninety years of age," the hermit added proudly, "and now I only await the time of my death."

Brendan and his companions listened to this tale in wonder. When the hermit had finished speaking, Brendan asked if they might replenish their water from the spring, and to this the old man agreed. "Be sure," he said, "that you will soon find your way to the Land of Promise, and that it shall be filled with all the wonders you desire."

THE LAND OF PROMISE

This time their course took them east and a few days later they encountered the great creature Jasconius. This time it seemed to act as a guide, leading them straight to the shores of the Island of Birds. Thus for the third and last time they saw the great tree and heard the delightful singing of the birds. And there, once again, came one of the birds, who had spoken to them twice before. It welcomed them and said: "You must prepare now for the final part of your voyage. This time I shall come with you, for you will not find your way to the Land of Promise without me. You have proved yourselves well in the time you have been upon this path, and now you shall have your reward."

The bird instructed them to take on provisions for forty days, and in the morning they set sail, the bird standing on the prow of the boat and guiding them.

Forty days exactly after leaving the Island of Birds they entered a thick mist.

"This mist surrounds the place you have been seeking," said the bird. "You must pass through it to find safe harbor."

The mist was like a curtain, but after a time it lifted and the voyagers found themselves looking at a wide land clad thickly with trees on which the fruit hung heavy. It seemed like perpetual summer in that place, and Brendan and his companions hastened to go ashore as soon as they might. The bird remained behind on the boat, saying that it was not yet time for it to go there.

So at last Brendan and his followers came to the Land of Promise, and they fell to weeping and embraced each other as old friends will who have shared so much together. What they found in that land can scarcely be set down in words. Food of the spirit and joy in abundance were theirs, and a sense of fulfillment. For in that place were health without sickness, pleasure without contention, union without quarrel, attendance of angels, feasting without end, meadows sweet with the scent of fair blessed flowers.

And indeed it was all just as the mariner Barinthus had told them. Like him, the companions wandered through a land of radiant light until they found themselves facing a great river, too wide to cross. There, as they stood upon the bank, came a youth who seemed covered with white down as a bird might be.

"Welcome," he said. "You have proved yourselves true to your intent and to the search for truth that led you to undertake this voyage. It is not yet time to cross this river, but you shall return one day and the way shall be open to you. For now, you may take of the fruit of this land, and any other riches you may find. You are blessed indeed, and will be honored in this land forever."

And so for a time Brendan and his companions remained in the Land of Promise, and learned much wisdom thereby. At the end of that period they took leave of the bird, who chose to remain behind. Then they set sail for home, trusting to the rhythms of the sea to carry them where they needed to go.

THE DEATH OF BRENDAN

Thus they came home, without further adventure, and were welcomed by all. As they spoke of their voyage and word of it spread, Brendan and his companions became famous throughout Ireland and Britain, and Brendan himself traveled about performing many miracles in the name of God.

And so the years passed until Brendan was ninety years old. One day when he was at a place named Enach Duin, there came to him a youth who was a bard and asked if he might play for the great man. At first Brendan would not let him, for he said that no music could be as fine as that he had heard in the Land of Promise and that he continued to hear every day in his inner thoughts. But at last he relented and the youth played some strains of music. As he listened, tears gathered in Brendan's eyes and rolled down his aged cheeks.

When the youth had finished, Brendan thanked him. "Now I know that my death is near," he said, "for this is the music I have longed to hear." And when he looked again the youth was nowhere to be seen.

Then Brendan called to the brethren who cared for him and told them that he would die in a few days. And so it was. Everything was done as Brendan had wished, and his remains were laid to rest in the shadow of a tree at Clonfert. Thereafter many miracles were performed in his name and all called him by the name of Saint Brendan. But of all the stories that are told of his deeds, none is better known, and rightly so, than that concerning his voyage in search of the Land of Promise.

⊠ ⊠ ⊠

They are not hard to identify with, these remarkable men who set forth blindly and with little idea of where they are going. All they know is that their leader has been "called" by God's angel to find a "secret country" that holds the prospect of wonder and blessing. But the journey is not that simple. On the way they will visit a number of islands—places that represent some of the stages on the soul's journey—and on each they will encounter something extraordinary, something that will change them forever. At the end of the voyage, when they return home, they are not the same people who left the shores of their own land in search of another.

Brendan himself is, from the start, gifted with inner certainty, a vision that not only makes him the natural leader of the company, but gives him insight into all that takes place. In this he is like that part of us all that is heard when we are in need of advice—the "still, small voice" that tells us what we must do. Of course, we do not always listen, but to ignore the inner prompting is to court missed opportunity. Thus the story speaks to us of trust—for Brendan must trust to his inner voice, just as his companions must trust to his leadership.

From the start the voyagers are guided by otherworldly agents: the unseen people who care for them on the Island of Hospitality; the wonderful bird who speaks to them on three occasions, offering help and guidance when they need it most; even the mighty beast Jasconius, on whose back they almost celebrate Easter and who later on guides them toward the end of their voyage. Nor should we forget the magical otter who has fed the hermit Paul with a fish every day of his thirty-year sojourn on a tiny islet.

There are human helpers too, the Ageless Elders and the mysterious angelic beings who appear at odd moments along the way to guide and advise the voyagers—just as, in our own lives, friends or helpers appear at opportune times to offer us the gifts of friendship and timely advice. Indeed we are more gifted than we realize with moments we may call synchronous: events that, often only retrospectively, we perceive as guiding our own voyage through life.

Again and again Brendan and his companions must give themselves up to the will of the waves, the rhythms of the ocean on whose back they sail, the guidance of the angel who, as Brendan says, is their navigator. It is these subtle rhythms, present also in the episode of the fish that seem to dance to a rhythm all their own, that offer us a pattern we can follow and learn from. We are like dancers ourselves, learning the steps and trying to follow the rhythm.

If one of the purposes of life is to find our appropriate course, then to be out of step with the universe is often a reason for our own failure to do so. Brendan and his companions constantly learn to accept the pattern that they are meant to follow—not slavishly and without freedom of choice, but simply by listening to and following the advice of those who have already been where they are headed and have experienced the difficulties of the voyage for themselves.

Often they are tested, just as we are, by the rigors of the journey. They, and we, must learn when to take what is offered and when to await permission: when to take only enough "food and water of the spirit" and when to be sensitive to the rhythms of the world in which we find ourselves, which has its own laws. We hear of the companions who drink too much of the water of the island and are lost in sleep as a result, of the man who steals the silver bridle and must pay the ultimate price for his action. Even here, the meaning is metaphorical as well as literal—to steal from life itself, for instance by deliberately warping a truth we recognize, is just as much a crime as actual theft from others in the outer world.

There are mysteries as well, for the world is full of wonders and not everything is meant to be understood—the Island of the Crystal Pillar, draped in the net through which it is hard to find a way, or the strange Island of Smiths, where the fierce occupants are threatening to the voyagers. These are left unexplained, but echo the mysterious adventures of the older voyagers, so that we know that they sail close to the borders of the Otherworld and are even able to look within for a moment. Such glimpses are as magical in our own lives as in the story—they are like the chinks of glorious light that sometimes pierce the soul's darker moments. They remind us also, *just as the mariner Barinthus was told, that the Land of Promise represents a state that we have experienced before, and that we can experience again, if we so desire.*

Throughout the story we are constantly told that the voyagers give themselves up to the rhythms of the natural world, for they are sailing the event horizon of creation where anything may happen and frequently does. The soul's journey is just as magical—just as fraught with adventure and mystery—as Brendan's voyage. From it we learn to see the inner light that illumines everything, that makes us part of the continuing unfoldment of creation. And, if we listen carefully enough, we may hear things within this story that speak to us at a deep level. Our own voyage may be only just beginning, or we may be nearing the harbor of the Land of Promise; but if we can learn to take soundings, to look about us with open eyes (how often do we think we see the truth only to find later on that we were wrong?), and to watch the water of the ocean on which we are sailing, we are far more likely to find clues to understanding the direction in which we are moving.

☒ ☒ ☒

Meditation Points

- Consider your own life as a voyage. Where are you at present: at the beginning, nearing the end, or somewhere in between?
- . What patterns are you aware of that have shaped your life?

- If you had to describe your own journey in terms of a voyage, what island points have you passed through to reach your current place?
- Draw a map charting the islands on your own *immram*. Give them names and a brief description of what took place there—for example: "The Island of Earthly Delights. Here I met my future life partner and we fell in love."
- Ask yourself: What, in my life, is the light that never fails? Do I listen to my own inner voice, or ignore it?

⬣ ⬣ ⬣

Columba's Song of the Ocean

Delightful would it be
To stand on a pinnacle of a rock—
That I might frequently see
The face of the ocean;
That I might hear the heaving waves
Chant their music to the Father;
That I might see the sparkling strand,
And hear the roar of the sea
By the churchyard wall;
That I might see flocks of birds
Over the tumultuous ocean;
That I might see monsters

The greatest of its wonders;
That I might see its ebb and flow
In their going and coming;
That I might bless the King
Who created all: land, strand, and flood;
That I might search my books
for the good of my soul;
At times on my knees
To the King of Heaven;
At times fishing,
At times giving food away,
At times in my solitary cell.

—*Attributed to Columba; translated by J. M.*

CHAPTER 2

THE BLACKBİRD'S CRY

KEVİN OF GLENDALOUGH

◼ ◪ ◼

Where Kevin was the eagles came
Down from the highest mountains, tame,
And sat among the lesser birds
To hear the wisdom of his words,
The speckled trout would swiftly glide
To the reedy water's side . . .

—*John Irvine*, Saint Kevin and the Wild Beasts

*The companionship of beast and bird, insect and fish, lies at the
heart of all Celtic spirituality, both pagan and Christian. Druids
and saints alike knew that one could learn from those that flew or
crawled, walked on four feet or swam in water. Creaturely trust
and fellowship were all-important aspects of the life and beliefs of
these early teachers, who regarded all living things as brothers and
sisters, all a part of one creation under heaven, and their simple
beauty a reflection of the beauty of the Otherworld.*

*As if in response to this the creatures themselves became guides
and helpers, just as they had been in the older, shamanic tradition,
where any creature, be it eagle or mouse, could be a great spiritual
teacher who had chosen this form for the sake of comfort and*

familiarity to those it helped. Again and again in the poetry of the times this is emphasized, as in this poem where a monk is inspired by the "learned music" of the lark:

> *Learned in music sings the lark,*
> *I leave my cell to listen:*
> *His open beak spills music, hark!*
> *Where heaven's bright cloudlets glisten.*

Living a solitary existence, the Celli Dé had time to listen, and were close enough to nature to appreciate both its terrors and its wonders. Saint Kentigern followed a hound and a robin to the place where he was to found his monastery; Piran of Cornwall founded a monastery in which the first monks were a fox, a badger, a wolf, and a doe; and Colman of Lindisfarne found support for his austere way of life from a cock, a mouse, and a fly. The cock and the mouse wakened him at prayer times, while the fly kept his place on the page he was reading whenever he was called away.

These are a remarkable enough testimony to the intimate relationship of human being and creature, but in stories of Kevin of Glendalough, who was born in Leinster around the middle of the sixth century, we find this magnified to a degree seldom equaled anywhere else. The site of the monastery he founded may still be seen, in the shadow of the Wicklow Mountains a few miles south of Dublin.

A Beautiful Shining Birth

Kevin was born of royal blood in the Fort of the White Fountain. His parents, Caemlug and Caemell, knew of a prophecy that spoke of the coming of one especially blessed, who would bring great goodness and well-being to the province of Leinster. But Caemell had no suspicion that it was to be her fourth son that would fulfill this promise, until, as she lay in childbed, she received a visitation from one of the Shining Ones who are called angels, who told her that she should give the name Coemgen, "beautiful, shining birth," to the son she would shortly bear, but that afterward he would have another name.

And so the child was born, an easy birth without pain, and when the day came for him to be baptized it was said that no less than twelve Shining Ones attended upon him, singing praises around him and prophesying his greatness; but his mother said afterward that she heard only the cry of a blackbird that flew into the church and sat in the rafters singing its own glorious song. Cronan, one of the holiest men in Leinster, performed the baptismal ceremony, and named the child Kevin, for that was the name of which the prophecy had spoken. And when the child's parents questioned him, Cronan closed his eyes and answered with this inspired verse:

This name, fashioned in heaven,
Shall cling to the child:

Believe, O woman of fair attendance,
that this shall be his given name.

Kevin's family took the baby home to the Fort of the White Fountain. The next day, as his mother sat with him at her breast, a white cow appeared, of great beauty, which had never been seen before. When she saw it Caemell knew that it had been sent by the Lady Brighid herself to feed her child. Every day thereafter for the next year it came, and Kevin drank of its milk until he was weaned, after which the cow vanished without a trace and was never seen again.

Thus Kevin grew until he was seven years old, at which time he saw a shining figure that spoke to him and told him to enter a monastery, where he might learn all that was required to become a wise and honorable teacher. Despite his youth Kevin convinced his parents that the message of the Shining One should be obeyed, and the serious child grew to be a serious youth among the monks, who grew to love him for his gentleness and kindness to all living things. It was at this time that he made many friends among the wild animals and birds that lived around the monastery. And often a solitary blackbird came and perched outside the window of his cell and sang to him.

One day the novice-master ordered Kevin to bring fire with which to light the candles in the church, and Kevin asked if he could have a vessel in which to carry the hot coals. For some reason the novice-master became angry at this, and ordered Kevin to carry them in the corner of his cloak. Without hesitating Kevin went away and returned shortly with several red-hot coals gathered into his mantle, and not even a scorch mark was there to see when he laid them by the altar. When he saw this, the novice-master said, "Indeed you are a child of wonder. I truly believe that all the prophecies that were made of you will be fulfilled."

LIFE IN THE WILD WORLD

Soon after this Kevin had a vision. A Shining One came to him and told him to go into a lonely place named Glendalough. Kevin did as his vision bade him, and found a cave in which to live. In time to come this place became known as "Kevin's Bed," because he had slept there.

This was a hard time for him, for he forsook the companionship of human beings utterly and lived in the wild, dressing in animal skins and sleeping on a stone bed. For food he ate nuts and herbs and other wild plants that nourished him. He had no fire to warm him, and often went to the lonely lake at the head of the valley and stood waist deep in the icy water for hours until he entered a state in which he saw the realm of the spirits clearly, and spoke with the Shining Ones and other beings, who were as real to him as any man or woman.

One day he sat by the edge of the lake reading from a most precious book of holy words that was his only possession. The cold numbed his hands and he let slip the book, which fell into the lake. For a while Kevin sat numbed with sorrow, then a sleek head broke the surface of the water. It was an otter, and in its mouth was his book. Kevin took it and opened it and saw that not a single word was blotted. He thanked the otter and thereafter always shared some of his food with it. Sometimes the otter brought him fish and then they would share this as friends will.

Always Kevin sought to live alone, as far away from people as he could. But he knew in his heart that one day he must return to the world of human beings and begin to teach the wisdom he had learned through living in the wild world.

One day he went to a part of the valley where there was a deep wood, and there he lived for a time, listening to the slow ancient voices of the trees and the songs of the birds that nested there. Here he heard the voice of the blackbird every day, and grew to know every note of its song. Then there came a day when he was lying in a hollow scarped in the bare earth, when a cow appeared suddenly at his side and began to lick his feet. Kevin laid his hands upon the gentle beast and drew close to share in her warmth.

Unbeknownst to Kevin the cow belonged to a farmer named Dimma, who pastured his animals in the forest and the surrounding land. At the end of the day the beast rejoined the rest of the herd and went home to Dimma's farm. There, to everyone's puzzlement, she gave as much milk as the rest of the herd put together. After this, every time the herd went to the forest the same cow would seek out the place where Kevin lay and remain with him throughout the day. And every time it was the same: the cow returned home and gave such generous portions of milk that everyone was astonished.

Finally, Dimma ordered his herdsman to follow the cow and see where it went. The man obeyed and found Kevin, lying thin and wasted from his life in the wild, barely able to stand or speak. Kevin so longed to be apart from other human beings that he begged the herdsman not to reveal his secret, and at first the man gave his word. But when he returned to the farm, Dimma questioned him so closely that in the end he gave way and told his master everything he had seen.

At once the farmer knew that this must be the holy man who was rumored to live in lonely Glendalough, and he swore that he would bring Kevin back to his house. "For surely he will bring good fortune upon us all," said Dimma. "It is not right that so good a man should live alone and neglected when he is so close to human habitation."

So the farmer called his children to him and they made a litter of tree branches and set off to the woods to find Kevin. When they did so, he was so weak that he could not stand, and so they lifted him into the litter, where he lay quietly and without complaint, having understood that the time was come for him to reenter the world.

On the way home the wood was so thick and impenetrable that they found it difficult to get through with the litter. But when Kevin saw this he prayed to the Shining Ones and the trees drew apart on either side until they had passed, only then resuming their former stance.

The Blackbird

Thus Kevin came to Dimma's farm and was nursed back to health and strength. And in return for his blessing and the wisdom he shared with everyone, the farmer built him a tiny cell in the woods, where he could live as he wished and where those who wished could seek him out. And indeed many came, as word of the holy man's wisdom spread throughout Leinster and beyond.

It was Kevin's habit to stand for long hours in his cell, with arms outstretched. And, because the wattled hut was so very small, this meant that both his hands were extended outside the tiny windows, made to let in the sun and the winds. One day as he sat thus, rapt in contemplation of the divine world, a hen blackbird flew down and landed upon one of his hands as if it were the branch of a tree. All day the bird stayed, and Kevin remained unmoving.

Next day it was the same, and this time the bird began to bring tufts of hair and grass and sticks with which to make a nest. A smile lit Kevin's face like the sun, and he remained perfectly still as the bird prepared her nest. Soon there were eggs in the nest, and still Kevin kept still, sleeping on his feet and eating only when pilgrims came to visit him. These he bade keep silent and watch the bird, in whose daily actions were contained all the mystery and wonder of the world. Thus he kept alive, sustained most often by his love of the world alone, until the eggs hatched and the chicks left the nest.

On that day one of the Shining Ones visited Kevin and told him that it was time for him to go out into the world and to build a foundation where others could come and learn. At first he resisted even this great demand, saying that he required longer to contemplate and learn the ways of all things. But the Shining One would brook no refusal, and so with reluctance Kevin came forth and began to seek those who would come together to form a community. Plenty there were who wished to share in his great wisdom and holiness, and soon there began to grow up in the lonely valley of Glendalough a monastery that would in time rival even Clonmacnoise. Indeed it was said that the four truly great places of pilgrimage in the whole of Ireland were the Cave of Patrick in Ulster, Croagh Patrick in Connacht, Inis na me-Beo (that is, the Land of the Living) in Munster, and Glendalough in Leinster.

So famous indeed did Kevin's foundation become that he was often hard-pressed to feed those who came there. Even the herd of sheep with which he was gifted by farmers from Leinster and beyond was scarcely enough. Then the day came when Kevin was forced to turn away some beggars who had come in search of food. But even as they were preparing to depart Kevin called them back. In the belief that a way would be found, he slaughtered the last few sheep in his flock and sent the beggars away happy. Next day the flock was renewed, exactly to the same number as before.

THE ⊙TTER'S TALE

Ever since the otter had brought back Kevin's book from the bottom of the lake, it had been wont to bring the gift of a fish. Every day it came to a certain point along the shore and left the fish for Kevin or one of his monks to find. Then one day it came no more, and Kevin went to the water's edge and called out to it to tell him why it had forgotten them. But the otter came not, and so Kevin went back to his church and prayed that he should be told what had happened to his faithful friend. Next day Cellach, the son of the farmer Dimma who had long ago brought Kevin from the forest, came and confessed that he had tried to capture the otter, believing that its skin would bring profit to the monastery. At once Kevin took the man back to the lakeside and made him promise, out loud, that he would never proffer harm to the otter or its kin, either then or at any time in the future. Next day the otter was back, and from then until the end of its days it continued to bring a fish for the monks.

THE DOE AND THE WOLF

The king of Ui Faelain had an ongoing struggle with an evil witch. Every child born to him was stolen away or destroyed by her, and there was nothing he could do to prevent it. Then, when a new child, a son, was born to him, he hit upon the idea of sending him to be fostered by Kevin of Glendalough, believing that the power of the holy man would protect his offspring against any dark magic.

As soon as the child was old enough to be baptized, his father sent him to Kevin. And on the day of his baptism, the dark witch came with her followers, their ragged black clothes whipping in a wind that none other could feel. When Kevin saw them coming he held up his hand against them, and they were at once turned to stone. To this day the stones may be seen clustered by the side of the lake.

So Kevin took in the infant son of the king, but at that time there were no cattle in the valley, and Kevin was concerned how he might obtain milk for the child. Then just as had happened long ago when the white cow came to feed Kevin himself, so now came a white doe and her fawn. Every day the doe would come to a certain hollowed-out stone, and there she would drop her milk for her own offspring, and for the king's son also, who thrived upon it.

Then one day a wolf came hunting, and caught and killed the fawn. Seeing this, Kevin bade the wolf offer no further threat to the doe, but to be quiet and lie down beside her as though it were her child. To the wonder of all the wolf obeyed, and the doe continued to drop her milk at the hollowed stone until it was no longer needed. And in time the king's son grew up and became one of Kevin's most devoted followers.

THE HUNTED BOAR

As time passed and the foundation of Glendalough grew in size and renown, Kevin sought often to return to his old hut in the wilds, often spending several weeks there before returning to the monastery. One day as he was sitting in the shade of the trees at the edge of the forest meditating upon the wonders of the world, there came a great crashing and crying in the wood and a wild boar burst out into the open and ran straight into Kevin's tiny cell. Almost at once a pack of savage hounds emerged from the trees in hot pursuit. When he saw them Kevin called out to them to stop, and at once their feet became stuck to the ground.

A few moments later the huntsman himself, a fierce man named Brandub who was known as a killer of animals and men for sport, came into view. When he saw the dogs standing still around the hut where the boar still sheltered, he raised his whip. Then he caught sight of Kevin, sitting quietly beneath the trees with birds fluttering around him and sitting on his head and hands. When the hunter's eyes met those of the holy man a change came over him, and he fell on his knees before Kevin and begged forgiveness for all he had done. Kevin forgave him, and the hounds were set free, and went off with their master as gently as lambs. The boar remained in the woods and often visited with Kevin from that time on.

And so the days turned to years and Kevin grew old. He lived long past the age reached by mortals at that time, and was loved and revered throughout the land of Ireland and beyond. The foundation at Glendalough became one of the most famous in all the Western world, and when Kevin died at last many hundreds of pilgrims came to pay their respects. But as many as there were of humankind, so too were there animals and birds who came to bear witness to the understanding of the saint. And it is said that a single blackbird sat upon his grave for many days, and visited it often thereafter.

❖ ❖ ❖

Animals were important in everyday Celtic culture, and a number of stories show that Kevin's relationship with animals and birds was a not uncommon tradition among older, pre-Christian figures. In some of the earliest Celtic traditions that have survived, we hear of tribal shamans who were either transformed into animals or possessed animal "helpers," otherworldly spirits who took the form of beasts, birds, or fish and were able to act as guides through their own particular element. In each case the shaman sought to take on the natural abilities of the creature itself: the strength of the bear, the speed of the hare, the keen-sightedness of the eagle or the hawk. By adopting the shape and consciousness of the creaturely, the shaman projected himself outside the normal range of human awareness, into a world where everything was different: more balanced, less complicated, less bound by the laws and mores of his own world. From here he could view the world of mortals and perceive it more clearly, with the kind of insights not generally available to him.

An early story that could easily have been told of Kevin relates how a man called Marvan possessed a white boar, which he declared to be "a herdsman, a physician . . . and a musician." When asked how this was possible, Marvan replied: "When I return from [herding] the swine at night, and the skin is torn off my feet by the briars of Glen-a-Scail, he comes to me and rubs his tongue over my foot, and he goes after the swine. . . . He is a musician to me, for when I am anxious to sleep I give him a stroke with my foot and he lies on his back with his belly uppermost and sings me a humming tune, and his music is more grateful to me than that of a sweet-toned harp in the hands of an accomplished minstrel." The boar, like most of the creatures mentioned in Kevin's story, was sacred to the Celts.

Animals were frequently twinned with human births, so that the resulting offspring became closely allied in later life. The Welsh hero Pwyll is stolen from his mother's side by a monster and left in a stable with a newborn colt, which afterward plays a significant part in his life. The fate of the Irish warrior Cuchulainn was linked with dogs (his name means "Hound of Culainn"), and it was only after he had been tricked into eating dog-meat that he was finally killed. It was also said of Cuchulainn that a mare dropped twin foals on the night of his birth, and that these became famous as the Black Saighlenn and Macha's Gray, with whom Cuchulainn had an almost symbiotic connection, and which arose from the depths of a lake at his call.

Another important role attributed to animals was their ability to provide inspiration, or to possess a knowledge of the past that far outstripped that of a human being. Some creatures were believed to live to very great ages, or were anyway of otherworldly provenance and thus possessed of wisdom deeper than that of mortals. In the story of "The Hawk of Achill," we see this as part of a theme known as "The Oldest Animals," where a number of creatures are consulted about various things and refer the questioner to successively more ancient beings.

In the story there is a wonderful dialogue between the wise Druid Fintan and the hawk of the title, part of which reads as follows:

Fintan:
Relate now, O bird of Achill,
The substance of your adventures;
For I am able finally
To converse in your tongue.

The Bird:
Though you seem still young,
It is long since you became shrunken,
In Dun Tulera washed by the sea,
O Fintan, O wise man.

Fintan:
O bird of Achill of the Fian,
Whom I have long desired to see,
Now that you are here indeed, tell me
Why you cleave to Achill?

The Bird:
O Fintan, never was there
A single night in Achill,
When I failed to obtain by my strength
Fish, game and venison.
O son of Bochra, speak fair,
And, since we are able to converse
Tell me of your life . . .

A similar poem, found in a medieval Irish manuscript, tells the
story of the White Blackbird. Enaccan, an old bard, asks a
blackbird what has whitened its wing down one side, and the bird
replies that it was Christ, who has kept it alive for longer than its
normally allotted span (we are not told why this should have
happened). The bird then proceeds to relate various events it has
witnessed in its long life.

He speaks of King Conchobar and the great gatherings of
the Ultonians in ancient days; of Queen Maeve and her
expedition on the Tain bo Cualnge. Far from him now was the
vigour of these gatherings, for he is older than Ross son of
Ruadh [tutor to Cuchulainn]. He has met with Oisin son of

Fionn, a man of wisdom. . . . He had witnessed the birth of
Christ in the flesh. Sweet was his song from the Wood of Cuan
when the host was destroying Troy. Many had been his
adventures since Bran went away on his ship. . . .
—The Book of Fermoy

The most important single factor in these stories is that the
protagonists are all carriers of tradition. They remember a past so
old that no human mind can encompass it. Nor is it just the facts of
history they relate, but the mysterious, inner tradition of the land.
In this way the past is kept alive and its representatives become
living containers for an accumulation of knowledge. Much of the
wisdom stored up in the lives of the Celtic saints is of this kind, and
like the older poetic and mythical stories to which they are akin,
they form an index to the traditions, rites, and beliefs of the Celtic
peoples.

There is much that we, too, can learn from the creatures we
encounter in our daily lives. Whether it is an interaction with a
beloved pet, a chance encounter with a creature in the wild, or a
face-to-face meeting with another species in a zoo, we may be struck
not only by the otherness of the being we face, but also by the links,
at a soul level, that connect us. From the very beginning of recorded
history an almost symbiotic relationship has existed between
humankind and the animal kingdom. The earliest representations
of animals in the cave art left behind by the Neanderthals show that
even in the pursuit of the creatures for food, the hunter took upon
him something of the nature of the creature itself. In shamanic

tradition all over the world the same intimate spiritual connection still holds true, and to a lesser degree the same holds good for our own relationship with our pets. Anyone who has looked into the eyes of dog or cat sees a mystery reflected back—something that extends beyond words, beyond even feelings, into the regions of the soul where all things share a common creaturehood. Even if we have never had a pet in our lives we may well find that a casual meeting with a bird or beast while out walking can have a deep and lasting effect upon us. The mind remembers a fleeting glimpse of a deer or stag, caught for a moment in the headlight of a car before leaping away. The heart understands birdsong better than the head, and responds with feelings of joy or sadness according to circumstance and song.

The kind of relationship described in the story of Kevin may be rare, but it is by no means impossible in our own time. The beasts who attended upon the saint felt the innate goodness of his soul; we do not need to aspire to holiness to extend the friendship of the soul to all creatures, and when we do so the rewards are great. For a brief time we can see with the eyes of the hawk, swim with the motion of the fish, hear the blood pounding in the heart of the stag. Again and again Kevin reaches out to a creature of fur, fin, or feather and is rewarded with a depth of response that is not hard to imagine. The strength, tenacity, grace, and beauty of all creatures are ours to access if we meet them on equal terms. This is the true meaning of the idea that humankind was given "dominion" over the animal world; not that we should dominate, command, or enslave as we have so often done in the past and continue, distressingly, to do today. Rather, the intent was that we should learn to live at one with our environment, of which the creatures are a hugely important part. When we are able to see this clearly, and to give up experimenting on living creatures, or enslaving them for food and well-being, we shall once again begin to experience the relationship that was once as natural as the sunrise to us all. At a personal level we can do this already, by simply tuning in to the creatures who share our planet and coming to terms with the fact that they are just as important as we are.

✶ ✶ ✶

Meditation Points

- Consider any animal, bird, fish, or insect with which you have had a direct encounter. How did this feel? Were you afraid, angry, loving, awed?
- If you have pets and do not already do so, spend some time interacting with them every day at a specific time.
- Consider what it might feel like to be an animal living in the wild.
- Now consider what it might feel like to be a domesticated animal, whether in the home or on the farm.
- Ask yourself what you can do to change the lot of any creature that is suffering from the actions of our own species.

⌘ ⌘ ⌘

Pangur Ban

I and Pangur Ban my cat,
'Tis a like task we are at:
Hunting mice is his delight
Hunting words I sit all night.

Better far than praise of men
'Tis to sit with book and pen;
Pangur bears me no ill will,
He too plies his simple skill.

'Tis a merry thing to see
At our tasks how glad are we,
When at home we sit and find
Entertainment to our mind.

Oftentimes a mouse will stray
In our hero Pangur's way;
Oftentimes my keen thought set
Takes a meaning in its net.

'Gainst the wall he sets his eye
Full and fierce and sharp and sly;
'Gainst the wall of knowledge I
All my little wisdom try.

When a mouse darts from its den
O how glad is Pangur then!
O what gladness do I prove
When I solve the doubts I love!

So in peace our tasks we ply,
Pangur Ban, my cat, and I;
In our arts we find our bliss,
I have mine and he has his.

Practice every day has made
Pangur perfect in his trade;
I get wisdom day and night
Turning darkness into light.

—*Verses written on the border of a ninth century manuscript;*
trans. Robin Flower

CHAPTER 3

All the
Bright Blessings
Brighid of Kildare

❈ ❈ ❈

The genealogy of the holy maiden Bride,
Radiant flame of gold, noble foster-mother of Christ.
Bride the daughter of Dougal the Brown,
Son of Aodh, son of Art, son of Conn,
Son of Criara, son of Cairpre, son of Cas,
Son of Cormac, son of Cartach, son of Conn.

—*Genealogy of Bride from*
The Carmina Gadelica

Arguably one of the greatest spiritual figures of early Ireland,
Brighid lived a life marked out by divine fire. Again and again we
hear of a burning light that surrounded her or gathered above her
head. Even her name has been interpreted as deriving from brea-
aigit, *"fiery arrow." The facts about her life can be briefly*
summarized, but her influence is far-reaching. As a woman in a
world dominated by men—as much in spiritual circles as secular—
she was a powerful influence on both men and women. Indeed, it
has been often noted that one of the truly original aspects of Celtic

Christianity was its openness to the feminine. A ninth-century text, the Catalogue of the Saints in Ireland, *makes this clear when it says that the founders of the Celtic church "did not reject the service and society of women." Brighid herself founded one of the first "double" monasteries at Kildare, where men and women lived in separate, adjacent quarters and came together in a single church to worship. There were a number of such foundations in Britain and Ireland at this time, and more than two hundred women saints are listed in the life of Gorman, the oldest female saint of whom we have any knowledge.*

Brighid herself was born in the province of Leinster and lived from about A.D. 452 to 524. Called "the Mary of the Gael" in token of her importance, she inherited many aspects of one of the great goddess figures of the Celts, Brighid, who was the deity of poetry, smithcraft, and the hearth. It may have been this association that promoted the numerous references to fire in her story, and she shared her feast day, February 2, with the earlier figure. Her followers kept an eternal flame burning in the monastery she founded at Kildare, a custom properly inherited from an older college of Druids who had occupied the site before her. In our own time these fires, which were only finally extinguished during the sixteenth-century Reformation, have been relit by women of many different cultures and beliefs, so that even now the eternal flame of Brighid's hearth is burning to fuel our own voyages in search of inner light.

Brighid is a supreme example of the kind of crossover between traditions that occurred during this time, a linking of the old and new beliefs, which frequently existed side by side and in harmony.

The earliest version of Brighid's life, on which the following story is based, makes it clear that Druids and Christians had far more in common than is generally understood, and that there were evident parallels in their approach to spirituality.

Brighid's compassionate nature, her openness to other kinds of belief, and above all, the burning passion of her spirituality make her one of the most important characters of the Celtic world. Known in Scotland as Bride, in Ireland as Brighid, in Wales as San Ffraid, in Britain as Brigantia, she is the major exemplar of the marriage of the old and the new, the pagan and the Christian. Her story is about offering the entire harvest of a life lived to the full, of a love expressed for every part of creation.

⊠ ⊠ ⊠

An Arrow of Fire

There was a nobleman in Leinster called Dubhthach who acquired a bondwoman named Broetsech. She was gentle and pretty, so that Dubhthach evinced a liking for her and took her to his bed. Soon after, it became evident that she was with child, and when Dubhthach's wife learned that he was the father of the child, she was not best pleased.

"Get rid of her," she said, "for I fear that one day her seed shall rule mine."

Dubhthach was unwilling to do this, for he had come to love Broetsech, but his wife made it clear that she would not let the matter rest. Then, while he struggled with the decision that must be made, an event took place that changed everything.

One day Dubhthach rode out in his chariot with Broetsech at his side. As they went they happened to pass the house of a certain Druid who, when he heard the chariot coming, asked his servant to go out and discover who it was that was coming. "For I believe it is a king who comes."

When the servant returned and told him that it was only Dubhthach, the Druid came out to look for himself. When he saw the bondwoman standing beside Dubhthach he looked at her with the eye of vision and asked, "Are you with child?" When Broetsech admitted that she was, the Druid asked, "And who is the father?"

"It is I who am the father," answered Dubhthach.

"Then take great care of this woman, for she has conceived a wondrous child."

"My wife wants me to sell her," said Dubhthach, "fearing that her seed shall be greater than her own."

"That is true," said the Druid. "Her children shall serve the children of this woman in generations to come. But do not fear," he went on, speaking to Broetsech. "Soon you shall give birth to a daughter whose radiance shall outshine the sun. No one shall harm you or your child, for there is a strong protection about you that none may overcome."

Now Dubhthach was even more determined not to sell his bondwoman, despite the pressure that both his wife and her brothers brought upon him. And so matters continued until one day it happened that a poet of the O'Neills was staying in Dubhthach's house, and when he learned something of the anger that was between Dubhthach and his wife, he offered to buy Broetsech and to care for her.

"Very well," said Dubhthach with a sigh. "But understand this: the child in her womb is mine, and belongs to me."

So Broetsech went home with the poet, who treated her well enough. Then one day soon after, a Druid came to stay in the poet's house, and he awoke in the middle of the night and saw that over the bondwoman stood a pillar of flame that lit up the night until it was as bright as day. No one else saw this, but next morning the Druid came to the poet and asked if he might buy the bondwoman from him. The poet agreed, but said: "The child she will bear belongs to Dubhthach of Leinster. See that no harm comes to it."

"Of that you may be certain," said the Druid.

Broetsech went with him that same day, for it was evident that she must soon bring forth her child, but at this time she was still able to travel.

Now it happened that soon after this the Druid made a great feast, and invited the king of Connaught and his queen, who herself went heavy with child. And that night at the feast the king asked when might be an auspicious time for his queen to bear their son. The Druid looked into the place within and said: "If she gives birth before sunrise, neither within nor without this house, the child she bears will grow to be among the greatest in all of Ireland."

But as it happened the queen came to her term that very night, and the child she bore was stillborn. But in the morning, when Broetsech was returning from the milking parlor with a pail of fresh milk, she had only put one foot across the threshold when she fell down and there and then gave birth to her child. The Druid's servants came to help her, and they bathed the child in the milk that her mother had but lately drawn. And some say that the baby was taken and laid next to the queen's dead son, and that he began to breathe at that moment; but whether this is true or not I cannot say, only that Broetsech's child was passing fair to look upon, and that from the moment of her birth she seemed to shine with a light that was not of mortal origin.

First Miracles

So for a time Broetsech and her child continued to live under the Druid's roof. Once the bondwoman had recovered from her lying-in she returned to her duties. So it was that one day she went out to the milking and left her daughter sleeping in the house. Passing neighbors saw the house in flames from ground to roof and ran for help. Yet when they returned with water there was no sign of any fire and the child slept peacefully in her cradle. The Druid, when he heard of this, said that it showed how the child burned with an inner fire that would one day be seen throughout Ireland. Soon after that he dreamed a dream in which three shining figures came and baptized the child in the name of Brighid, which means "fiery arrow." When he told her mother this, the bondwoman declared that thus would she name her child, and the Druid said that since the Shining Ones themselves desired it, so it should be, and that her name was a fortelling of her life.

Thereafter the Druid took an especial interest in the child, and watched her often. He noticed, as did all, that as she grew so she ate less. Whatever was put before her from the Druid's table she could not stomach, but vomited it up. When he saw this the Druid looked into the place within and declared that the child should take milk from a certain red-eared cow in his herd, and bade a woman named Christina to milk it daily and to be Brighid's nurse thereafter. This milk Brighid was able to take, and afterward grew daily more hale and strong.

As time passed Brighid began to ask about her father, and learning that he was the noble Dubhthach, she wished to go and see him. The Druid sent word and, filled with pride when he heard of the extraordinary nature of his daughter, Dubhthach came to take her home to Leinster. On the journey Brighid's nurse, who had come with her, fell ill. Hearing of a certain lord who was holding a great feast nearby, Brighid and another girl in the party went to beg some ale for the sick woman. The lord refused them. Brighid therefore went to a nearby well and having drawn water, said a blessing over it, at which it took on both the appearance and taste of ale. She took this back to the sick woman, who began to recover as soon as she drank. But as to the lord's feast, when they opened the barrels of ale that had been set aside for it, they were found to be dry.

Amazed and somewhat bemused by this evidence of his daughter's wondrous gifts, Dubhthach gave her the task of looking after the swine. One time when he was away robbers came and stole two of the pigs. By chance Dubhthach encountered them upon the road and was able to take back what they had stolen. When he returned he put the pigs into a pen of their own; then he went to Brighid and said, "Are all the swine safe?" Brighid looked at him solemnly and said, "Do you go and count them, Father." And when Dubhthach did so there was exactly the right number.

Whatever Brighid did seemed to turn to increase. Once when Dubhthach had a noble guest he gave to his daughter the task of preparing a meal. She was given five strips of bacon to cook, and set about it while the guest nodded before the fire. She had scarcely begun when a poor hungry hound entered the house and begged for food. Brighid at once gave it one of the strips of bacon and, when that was not enough, a second strip. Soon Dubhthach came and asked her if the supper was ready. Brighid laid out five strips of bacon for the guest, who looked with wonder upon the feast. Then he told Dubhthach how he had seen the girl feed the hungry dog. After that, neither felt like eating the food but instead gave it to be shared among the poor.

Soon after this Brighid returned to the Druid's house to see her mother, and found Broetsech ill with a fever. The bondwoman's task at that time consisted of looking after the dairy and making butter for the household. Brighid took over this task with a will and performed her duties so well that the amount of butter produced by the dairy more than doubled. The Druid decided to discover if this was another of the girl's miraculous works, so he took a huge basket to the dairy and asked Brighid if she could fill it. Now at that moment she had only enough to fill a quarter of the basket, but she went into the kitchen and uttered a charm over the butter.

O great prince,
Who can do everything,
Bless, O God,
My kitchen with your right hand.

My kitchen,
A kitchen of the White God
A kitchen my King has blessed—
A kitchen filled with butter!

The Druid heard this and wondered. When the girl came out to him she had enough butter to fill another third of the basket, but somehow, when she placed it inside, it grew to fill the whole. When he saw this the Druid said, "Truly you are most wondrous." Then he offered to give her cattle for her own. But

Brighid shook her head. "I have no need of cattle, but if you wish to reward me, then give my mother her freedom."

The Druid answered, "It shall be as you wish. But you shall have the cattle also, and anything else that I can spare."

Thus Brighid and her mother returned home to Leinster and to her father's house. And at first all was well with them. But then there came a suitor who desired to marry Dubhthach's daughter and he was more than willing. But Brighid said that she would never marry, since she had other work to do. Dubhthach was angry at that and threatened to sell her, since by law she was still his property. But Brighid looked at him and said, "If you force this upon me I shall pluck out my eyes, for I will never be wife to any man!" Such was the fire in her then that Dubhthach could not gainsay her, and soon after he gave her her freedom.

BRIGHID THE ABBESS

For a time Brighid and her mother lived together, eking out their livelihood from the cattle the Druid had given them. Then one day Brighid announced that she intended to join a community of holy women in Telch Mide. "For I have seen that I have work to do in this world, and thus will it begin."

So Brighid went to Bishop Mél who, having heard something of her remarkable abilities, was glad to welcome her. It is said that on the night before she arrived, the bishop dreamed a dream of the Mother of God, and that when he saw Brighid face-to-face she bore the same appearance as the woman in his dream. For this reason, it is told that Brighid in after years was known as the Mary of the Gaelic people.

When the day appointed for her to take the veil arrived, Brighid waited with several other women who were all to dedicate themselves to the service of God. When Brighid's turn came it happened that the prelate read out the wrong form of words over her, namely that for an abbess. When it was realized what he had done there was an instant outcry, for many present believed that a woman could not hold so high an office. But at that moment they all saw a column of flame enfold Brighid, and in awe Bishop Mél declared that a higher authority than his had chosen Brighid for this role.

Thus it came about that Brighid became an abbess, though she was scarcely twenty-two years old and had as yet no foundation or following. Yet word of the wonders that followed her quickly spread. It was told how she cured lepers and the blind, and how a young boy who had been dumb from birth spoke when she asked him a question. Even her shadow was said to heal others, and water or milk blessed by her wrought miracles. Above all, it was the increase of all things that people spoke of. Whether sheep or cattle or pigs, food or ale or wheat, whenever there was an insufficiency of these things among any community in need, if Brighid came there it was sure to be sufficient and more.

And so it came to be that a large number of men and women sought her out, wishing both to be in her presence and to hear her teachings. When she saw this Brighid sent word to Bishop Mél asking him to come with her in search of a site on which she could build her own foundation. For a time they traveled together and found nowhere suitable. Then on a certain day as they were on the road they met a cavalcade of carts loaded with wood, which were destined for Ailill son of Dunlang. Now when Brighid saw this she looked within and listened to the voice of an unseen companion. When she had heard all there was to hear she went to Ailill and asked if she might have some of the wood with which to build at a spot near there.

"Not so much as a stick will I give to you," Ailill declared. As he spoke all the carts came to a halt in the road and the horses could not take another step or be moved by any means. When he saw this, Ailill bowed to Brighid and begged her to take all the wood she wished.

Thus the building began at a place nearby, which was known as Kildare, and which had previously housed a community of Druids. Brighid was especially glad to be here, feeling the commonality of all beliefs, and here she founded her first community, which was to become one of the foremost in all Ireland. And the first thing that Brighid caused to be done, when the building was complete, was the lighting of a fire on the chief hearthstone of the foundation, and when it was alight she said, "May this light burn forever in the world and may it never be allowed to go out." And both while she was alive and for many years after her death the fire was tended in such a way that it was never extinguished.

THE WOUNDED HEALER

Not long after this Brighid fell ill, being affected by a disease of the eyes and headaches that made her unable to stand. Bishop Mél came to her and would have taken her to a famous healer who lived some way off. They set forth, Brighid riding with difficulty. Along the way Brighid became dizzy and fell from the horse's back onto the road. Her head struck a stone and the wound bled profusely. She was helped to mount again and they continued on until they reached the place where the healer lived. When he saw the abbess, he said that there was no greater source of healing than herself, and that he could do nothing for her. When he spoke these words the sickness left Brighid and she was as hale as ever—though afterward it was said that she saw things in the inner worlds more clearly than before and was herself an even more powerful healer.

On the way back to Kildare Brighid and the bishop stayed for a night in the house of the king of Teffia. It happened that a servant broke a most precious cup that belonged to the king, for which he was thrown into prison. When Brighid heard of this she asked that he be set free, but the king refused her. "Then give me the shards of the cup," requested Brighid.

"Those you may have," said the king.

When Brighid took them in her hands and breathed upon them they were restored as if they had never been broken. "Thus is the life of the soul," Brighid said. "Though it may be easily broken yet it may be restored." At this the king sent word to release his servant and he became a devoted follower of Brighid thereafter.

This was not the only time that Brighid saved a condemned man. Once when she was in the district of Fir Rois she heard of a man that had been imprisoned for no good reason. She begged the local king for his release. "Not though you offered me the sun and the moon," said he. "But so that you shall not go from here with a refusal, I give you the care of his soul for one night."

At that Brighid smiled and went to the man in prison. There she taught him some words of blessing and said to him, "When you say these, your chains shall fall from you." Wondering, the man did as he was bid and the chains fell from him. "Now," said Brighid, "repeat the words once more, and when you do so the locks that hold you shall open." Again the man did as Brighid said, and the locks of his cell opened at once. "Now go home," said Brighid, and the man departed and was seen no more in that part of the country.

The Midwife of God

Brighid's fame continued to spread, and many more tales are told of her wondrous works. On one occasion it is said that when seven holy men came to visit her, there was insufficient milk to feed them all, for the cows had already been milked that day. But one of the Shining Ones that are called angels came to Brighid and told her to milk the cows again. When she did so, they gave enough milk for her guests, and moreover the milk continued to flow from the pails in which it was put so that a river of milk spread out and formed a lake. This may still be seen today and is known still as the Lake of Milk.

Another time a foolish churl in the service of the king of Leinster killed a tame fox that was much beloved of his lord, and that had been taught various tricks. When the king heard what had happened he commanded that the man be thrown into prison. "Unless a fox as wise and skillful as mine comes to the court in the next few days," the king declared, "both this man and all his family shall be sold into slavery."

When word of this came to Brighid she at once called for her chariot to be brought and set out for the king's court. As she went she called aloud to all the creatures of the world to send her help. Soon there came a wild fox that ran beside her and finally jumped up and hid beneath her cloak. Thus Brighid came before the king and asked for the man to be set free. The king repeated his oath, and at that Brighid opened her cloak and the fox jumped out and began to dance and do tricks just as the old one had done. When he saw that, the king was well pleased and set free the man and his family, who went home with Brighid. Afterward, when they were safely away, the fox ran off and returned to the wild.

But one story is told that is a greater mystery than all the rest. For it is said that by some miraculous shifting of the shape of time Brighid was permitted to pass for a time into the age when the Lord of the Elements was born. And it is told that she was at the lying-in of Mary, and acted as midwife to the Child of Wonder. Whether this be a true tale or not I cannot say, but it is told still in Ireland and many there believe it to be so.

At length the ending of her days came upon Brighid. Her last act was to ask again that the fires that burned on the hearthstones of Kildare be kept burning perpetually in token of the fires she had lit in the hearts of so many. And thus it was done, and thus it continues to be done even to this very time.

Many came to look upon her body and to honor her. And no lesser person than Columbcille himself made a song over her that is still said to this day. And it is further said that when years after he was in danger upon the sea and spoke the words of his hymn aloud, the waters were calmed. This is the song that he made:

Brighid, excellent woman, flame of the sun,
golden, delightful, radiant as the stars—
may her dazzling light guide us to the long home,
may she save us from all harm,
may she fight our battles against disease.
may the gentle rain of her spirit fall upon us!

Brighid's story is about compassion and continuity—the compassion for all things that she constantly exhibits, and the continuity of belief and tradition that is borne out in the story of her birth and upbringing in the house of the Druid.

Her ancient origins as the goddess of poetry, smithcraft, and the hearth fire are borne out again and again in the traditions that have grown up around her, and that are specifically applied to her Christian form as well as her pagan aspect. One of the most important and startling of these associations is with divination. The "augury" or frith *(pronounced* free*) of Brighid grows out of the tradition that makes her the midwife and foster mother of Christ and the perpetual helper and friend of Mary. The Gaelic method of the* frith *was said to derive from the loss of Christ by Mary in the Temple. Brighid searches for the lost child by making a* frith *between her hands. This is recorded in an ancient text:*

> *The Frith that Brighid made for her Fosterling,*
> *Making a pipe within her palms:*
> *"I see my Fosterling by the well-side,*
> *Teaching the people without doubt.*
>
>
> *I made my frith towards the well*
> *And that was the best way of working:*
> *The King of Kings teaching the people,*
> *I see my Christ down there certainly."*
> *—Trans. Caitlín Matthews*

This method of curling the hands to form a "seeing-tube" seems originally to have been used by frithirs (pronounced freer) to find lost people and animals, or to discover the health of an absent being. Among the Irish Gaels the use of the palms is widespread, to provide a "seeing-space" or tabula rasa, to block out the light, or to focus the seer. The usual practice of the frith was undertaken by the frithir, fasting, on the first Monday of the quarter, at sunrise, with bare head and feet. It was made in order to divine the portent for the coming quarter. Special prayers to invoke Mary and Brighid and to welcome the frith were said while walking deasil (clockwise) around the household fire three times. Then, with closed or blindfolded eyes, the frithir went to the threshold of the house, placing one hand on either jamb and praying to be granted the request that had occasioned the frith. Finally, with open eyes, she looked steadfastly ahead and noted all that she saw.

The signs are called rathadach (lucky) and rosadach (unlucky). A man or beast rising up indicates improving health, or ill-health and death if lying down. A cockerel coming toward the frithir is fortunate, whereas other approaching birds indicate news. A duck indicates safety for sailors; a raven portends death.

The maintaining of the eternal flame of Kildare is central to an understanding of Brighid's place in Celtic tradition. It is more than a symbolic act, being a very profound connection to her own "fiery" nature and to the links in a chain of continuity that flow out of her dual-aspected identity. A ninth-century hymn to Brighid makes a clear reference to this, as well as to the dating of her feast day, which marks the diminishing of winter and the coming of spring at

*the ancient Celtic festival of Imbolc on the night of February
1st/2nd.*

> *I take Bride as my advocate.*
> *Dear to me is Erin,*
> *Dear to me each land,*
> *Praise be to it!*
>
> *O white flame of Leinster,*
> *Enlighten the whole land,*
> *Chief of Erin's maidens,*
> *Chief of finest women.*
>
> *Dark the bitter winter,*
> *Cutting its sharpness,*
> *But Brighid's mantle*
> *Brings spring to Ireland.*
> > *—Trans. Caitlín Matthews*

*Brighid's mantle (Bratach Bhrighid), also mentioned here, is
continually invoked in Ireland to protect people, beasts, and houses.
Midwives would leave out a special shawl on Imbolc Eve so that
Brighid would bless it: a shawl so blessed was placed around the
shoulders of laboring women to speed their delivery.*

*Brighid's story is one of infinite compassion and
openheartedness. She is unique among the saints in having been
brought up in the house of a Druid in whose company she found it
easy to be, and who himself saw and predicted much of her*

greatness. Her gifts are those of a generous spirit, and whatever she touched was bound to increase. She is of primary importance in the history of the Celtic saints in that she bridges the worlds between the older traditions and the new faith, and because she represents the importance of the feminine principle for both ancient and modern. As Bride she is a goddess of profound strength, teaching the gifts of poetry and smithcraft and the importance of maintaining the fires of the hearth. As Saint Brighid she becomes a repository of the fiery light of the divine, symbolized by the perpetual flame at Kildare, which was kept alight until the dawn of the Reformation.

This symbolism of fire, which threads all through her story like a bright gold thread, is what we may choose to remember her for today. It is the fire of inspiration, of divine insight, and of the rich heritage of the two traditions she spans. In Ireland she is still acknowledged as a patron of travelers, midwives, and healers. Her gifts in each of these areas are present in her story, which in its fullest form is an astonishing catalog of miraculous cures. The story of her presence at the birth of Christ is one of the most astonishing, and connects to a number of stories in Celtic tradition suggesting that the Druids as well as others were aware of the appearance of a new aspect of universal deity.

The message Brighid holds out to us is one of the importance of continuity, the honoring of past as well as present traditions, and the recognition that there are no breaks in the long history of spirituality. This, together with the protection she holds out to all, is borne out in a great invocation of Brighid that is found in the Hebridean tradition.

It begins:

Brigit of the mantles,
Brigit of the peats,
Brigit of the braided hair,
Brigit of the auguary.
(see also pp. 76–78)

It was said that if this prayer was repeated daily no harm
would come to the person who did so. In similar fashion, recalling
the eternal flames of Brighid's hearth at Kildare, Gaelic mothers
would breathe these words over the fire as it was banked in for the
night:

I smoor the hearth
As Brighid the Foster Mother would smoor it.
The holy name of the Foster Mother
Be upon the hearth and the herd,
Be upon each of my household.
          —Trans. Caitlín Matthews

As she said this, she would spread the embers into a circle, and
divide it into three equal heaps with a central heap. To make the
holy name of the Foster Mother, she placed three turfs of peat
between the three heaps, each one touching the center, and covered
it all with ash.

Thus the protection of Brighid is wrapped about the house and
its occupants, preserving the threefold integrity of the soul, and
enfolding it in the presence of the fires of inspiration and wholeness.

⊠ ⊠ ⊠

Meditation Points

- Consider the acts of compassion that you have performed in your life. What further acts might you do?
- What auguries might you make for your own life? For what would you ask?
- Consider how you can increase the bounty of your spiritual life.
- Whether you are a man or a woman, consider the importance of the feminine in spiritual practice.
- Ask yourself how you can combine the inner life of the spirit with the outer life of the world.
- What kind of fire illumines your life? What inspires you, and how can you find more of it in your day-to-day living?

⊠ ⊠ ⊠

Brighid of the Mantles

(*Sloinntearachd Na Brighid*)

Brighid, daughter of Brown Dugall,
Son of Aodh, son of Art, son of Conn,
Son of Criara, son of Cairpre, son of Cas,
Son of Cormac, son of Cartach, son of Conn.

Brighid of the mantles,
Brighid of the peats,*
Brighid of the braided hair,
Brighid of the augury.

Brighid of the shining feet,
Brighid of the quietness,
Brighid of the shining palms,
Brighid of the cattle.

Brighid, friend of women,
Brighid of the peats,
Brighid, women's midwife,
Brighid, woman of grace.

Brighid, tress of Mary,
Brighid, Foster-Mother of Christ;
Each day and each night
I say the Genealogy of Brighid:

I shall not die,
I shall not be pierced,
I shall not be imprisoned,
I shall not be ill-wished,

* *turf-fuel*

I shall not be riven,
I shall not be plundered,
I shall not be down-trodden,
I shall not be exposed,
I shall not be torn,
Nor will Christ
Be forgetful of me.

No sun shall burn me,
No fire shall scorch me,
No beam shall pierce me,
No moon shall blanch me.

No waters shall drown me,
No brine shall choke me,
No flood overwhelm me,
No stream shall drown me.
No vexatious word shall quell me,
No black slumber shall oppress me,
No drunken stupor fall upon me,
No quicken-ash spell lie upon me.

I am under the protection
Of Holy Mary;
And my dear companion
Is Brighid.

—*Trans. Caitlín Matthews*

CHAPTER 4

THE WISDOM OF WILD WORDS

COLUMBA OF IONA

◼ ◼ ◼

Behold Iona!
A blessing on every eye that see it!
He who does good for another here,
Will be repaid a thousandfold!

—*Attributed to Columbcille*

Columba, or as he is more properly called, Columbcille, is rightly deemed one of the greatest of the Celtic saints. His wisdom, recorded sometimes in his own words, is warm and joyful, and the events of his life are as remarkable as those of any of the others who appear in this book. Indeed, there is so much that one might gainfully learn from his life that it was difficult to know what to put in and what to leave out.

Born at Gartan, a wild district in Donegal, on December 7, 521, of royal stock, Columbcille was educated by the great Finnian of Clonard, who also had Ciaran as a pupil (see chapter 8). Between 546 and 599 he founded a number of important monasteries, including those at Derry, Durrow, and Kells. In 580 he took part in an assembly at Druim-Cetta, where he argued in favor of the bardic community of Ireland and was thus largely responsible for saving it from extinction.

But most famously he is known as the founder of a community on the tiny island of Iona in 563, where he settled after being driven into exile—why is not known—from Ireland. He remained there for the rest of his days, making only occasional forays into Ireland, where he kept a kind of overlordship from afar. From the tiny island to the southwest of Scotland, given to him by the king of the Irish Dalraida, Columbcille radiated wisdom and strength of purpose. He was known as a fine poet and a brilliant scholar, and several surviving works are attributed to him, though none with certainty. His biographer, Adamnan, describes him vividly as tall, powerfully built, and possessed of a commanding presence. Just but never overly harsh, he gave himself single-handedly to the creation of the foundations of wisdom for which he is famed. His whole life was dedicated to learning and a passion for the truth, which shines forth in every line of his life. He saw the need for education among the people whose spiritual lives he oversaw, and dedicated much of his life to the furtherance of the skills of reading and writing. He was also a visionary whose prophecies are an astonishing catalog of events bearing on the inner history of the Celts in Ireland.

Whatever the reason for his exile, it obviously meant a great deal to Columbcille. A poem attributed to him puts these feelings across in words drenched with the pain of homesickness:

How delightful it would be,
O Son of Mary,
To cross the sea,
The well of floods,
To Ireland.

To Mag nEolairg by Benevanagh,
Across Loch Foyle where
The harmony of swans
Would offer comfort to me. . . .

To listen early in Ross Grencha
To the call of the stags;
To hear the cuckoos calling
From the brink of the summer woods.

I have left three things
I loved the best:
Durrow, Derry, and Tir Luigdech—
I have loved the lands of Ireland.

This is the voice of a man who loved the world as much as he
loved the places of the soul; whose long and sometimes difficult
journey never ceased to burn with the light of inspiration and a deep
love for all created things.

THE FORETELLING OF THE DOVE

Decades before his birth Columba's coming was predicted—
first by a wise man named Maucta, who said: "In the last ages
of the world [as it was deemed in those days] a son shall be
born who shall be called Columba, and whose name shall be
known in every corner of these islands. Bright as a star shall he
shine and all men shall recognize his wisdom."

Long after this, in the time of Conall Gulban son of the
great hero Niall of the Nine Hostages, it happened that Conall
was hunting one day near Gartan in the province of Derry.
And though his hounds several times raised and cornered
game, each time they turned away and would not kill it.
Conall marveled greatly at this, and on returning home consulted his Druids concerning it. They told him that a child
would be born to the third generation hence of his line, and
that it would be a marvelous child, and because it was to be
born in that place where he had been hunting so the hounds
had spared the game in token of the future peacemaker whose
name would be Columba.

These things were recorded in the books of the wise, and
when Columba was born many recalled them and knew that a
rare being had come into the world.

Fedlimid, son of Fergus, son of Conall Gulban, son of Niall
of the Nine Hostages, and Ethne the daughter of Dima, who
was descended from Cathair the Great, were his parents.
While she was great with child Ethne had a dream in which

she was given a great cloak. So vast was this garment that it
stretched over much of Ireland and Scotland, as well as the
seas between; and it was made up of every color imaginable,
woven in shifting patterns of light. In her dream a youth of
radiant beauty came and took the cloak from her and this
made Ethne sad. But the youth spoke to her and gave her comfort. "Lady," he said, "you have no need of sorrow, for the
meaning of this cloak is that your son, who shall be born into
the world soon, shall send forth his light over Ireland and
Scotland, and everyone shall acknowledge the wisdom of his
words." And as Ethne awoke, she seemed to hear the voice of
the youth bidding her to name her child Columba, which
means "dove" in the Celtic tongue.

Soon after that, Ethne's time came upon her, and it is said
that she went into the wilderness and brought forth her child
alone and unaided. Some say also that she brought forth a red
stone at that time, and that in after years it was seen to perform miracles of healing. But whether this is true or not, there
was no doubting that the child was marked out from the
beginning to be special.

In accordance with the custom of the time he was given
into the care of fosterage. The one chosen for this task was
named Cruithnechan, a wise and generous man who was
skilled in learning. From the start he declared the child to be
quick and adept at all things, and said that he displayed a wisdom far beyond his years. One night, coming home late,
Cruithnechan saw the sleeping Columba surrounded by light of

such brilliance that he could scarcely bear to look upon it. From this, as from other signs, he knew that the boy was filled with a special power, and to Ethne and Fedlimid he declared his intention of placing him in the care of the wise and noble Finnian, who was a tutor to many of the greatest of the *Celli Dé*.

Soon after this, as he lay abed, it seemed to Columba that a shining being came to him and wished him well.

"Who are you?" asked Columba.

"I am your guardian," answered the Shining One. "Wherever you go I shall walk with you and be your guide."

Columba's eyes opened wide. "What is your name?" he asked.

"You may called me Axal, which means 'helper,'" answered the Shining One. And thus it was that even before he had entered upon the course of his life Columba learned that he was to be guided and protected in all that he did.

Columba at Clonard

So Columba went to Clonard, and was welcomed by Finnian, who already knew that he was to be a remarkable pupil. Indeed, it was at this time that Finnian had the vision in which he saw the moon and the sun rise in the sky at the same time, and the moon went and stood over the northern part of Ireland and over Scotland, while the sun went and stood over the center of Ireland. And as has been told elsewhere (in chapter 8), the significance of this sign was that the sun stood for

Columba and the moon for Ciaran and for the great deeds they would do in these lands.

Now it was the custom that each new pupil at Clonard should build his own hut, in which he would live while he was there. Columba asked Finnian where he should build his. "Put it by the door of the church," replied Finnian, "for I see that you shall yourself be a doorway to many." But when Columba built his bothy it was not outside the door of the church but some way to the left, and only in later years was the building extended in such a way that the door stood precisely where Columba had lived. It may well be that this was the first sign of the prophetic ability that Columba was to display so markedly in his life.

Columba remained at Clonard for a time, and learned much wisdom from Finnian and enjoyed the company of his other pupils, including Ciaran, who became his soul-friend thereafter, and others who were to establish many great houses of wisdom in Ireland.

When Columba had been at Clonard only a few years, it is told that a plague came upon the land, and that Finnian sent his pupils away to ensure their safety, though he himself would not leave. Columba went on his way to his home at Gartan, and when he reached the stream known as the Bir, he blessed its waters. The plague continued to spread through the land unchecked until it came to the banks of the Bir and there it stopped and came no farther because of the power of Columba.

Columba in the Oak Groves

Soon after came word of the death of Finnian, and Columba mourned his old friend and teacher greatly. Yet he said also: "This is the sign that I have awaited. For now I must go and teach the ways of God throughout Ireland." And thus he began to follow the wandering way, traveling to every part of the land and sharing his learning and wisdom with all who would listen. In time he came to the place called Derry, and there he founded his first great school. Ever after he spoke of this place as especially dear to him, for it was possessed of the oak-knowledge of an older time (indeed the name Derry comes from the word for oak in the tongue of Ireland). Of this place Columba was to write:

> For this reason do I love Derry:
> For the smoothness of its hills,
> for the purity of its airs,
> And because it is filled with shining angels
> From one end to the other.

But the first days in that place were not easy for Columba and his followers. For when he ordered some trees to be felled to begin building the monastery, a certain warrior on whose lands they were became angry that Columba had not asked his consent before beginning the work. When he heard this, Columba said: "Take the worth of the wood in barley-grain and tell the warrior to plant it at once." Now it was close to midsummer at the time, long past the time for planting. But though the lord scorned the offering, yet he planted it, and it grew and was ripe in time for harvest nonetheless, so that thereafter the warrior troubled Columba and his followers no more.

So for a time Columba continued to travel about Ireland, until it chanced that he angered one of the kings of that land, who ordered him sent into exile. Many said that he should stay, but rather than cause trouble in his beloved land, Columba chose to depart. "It seems to me," he said, "that another place awaits me." And with a small company of his closest followers he set sail forthwith for the land of Scotland. But before he was to set foot upon that shore his ship was drawn away by tide and current until it landed upon an island called Hy. Today this place is known as Iona and is regarded as sacred by all who set foot upon its soil. Here Columba knew that he had found a place that would be home for him thereafter.

And so he set about building a place of shelter where all who wished might come to learn and share the wisdom he himself had begun to discover. But fast as they built, in the night there came a force that threw down all they had accomplished. At last one of his companions, a man named Odran, came forward and said, "Master, a vision has been granted to me. A deep disturbance is under the earth, and one of us must go there living before our foundations will stand. I wish it to be me." At first Columba would hear nothing of this, for it seemed to him a dark thing to do. But when two more nights passed and the work of the brothers was thrown down, he saw the truth of Odran's words. With much ceremony the brother was interred alive close to the center of the island, and from that night the foundations of the building remained untouched. But Columba could not rest. Every morning for the next five days he walked to the site of Odran's grave and returned full of sorrow. At length he could bear it no longer. "I must look one more time upon the face of Odran," he said. And so the brethren returned to the place where they had buried their companion and began to dig.

Soon they uncovered the simple coffin in which Odran had been interred. Columba himself opened the lid, and then it was that there occurred a strange and wondrous thing. For Odran opened his eyes and sat up! He looked at the brothers and into the eyes of Columba and spoke:

I have been where no living man has been,
And I must speak.
Heaven is not as we think,
Nor is Hell as we think;
Nor are the good eternally happy,
Nor the bad eternally sorrowful. . . .

He would have spoken more, but Columba held up his hand and ordered the brothers to depart. And indeed they were glad enough to leave, for they were fearful at Odran's words. But Columba remained there at the grave site for some time. Afterward, when he came away, the earth was back upon the tomb of Odran, and Columba never spoke of what he had heard. Ever after the place was known as Relig Odran, "the Grave of Odran," and all the brethren of the community who died were buried there.

After this the community grew apace, and though he traveled far afield in the years to come, Columba always returned to Iona, and because of him the island became a shining light for all the world. But though he learned to love the bright sky arching above the green earth and the bare rocks, Columba's heart ever yearned for the shores of Ireland, and in more than one poem that he wrote he expressed the deep yearning of his soul for his homeland.

COLUMBA'S PROPHECIES

Every day Columba used to have one of his followers give as much food as he could spare to the poor, and every day many came to receive his gifts. But one day a man came after all the rest and the brother whose task it was to give out the alms turned him away and told him to come again next day. On the morrow the same man came again, but once again he was too late and again the almoner turned him away. Then the man looked at the brother and said, "Go and tell Columba that he has more than enough to feed as many as will come here, and that he shall offer more than food for the body."

When he heard this, Columba jumped up and ran after the man without waiting to put on either his cloak or his shoes. When he overtook him the two fell in beside each other and spoke together for a time. But soon the man who had come begging vanished away and Columba returned home alone and silent. But from that day forward he was possessed of a gift that was both a blessing and a terror—the gift of inner sight, which caused him to see things that had yet to be or that took place far away. Again and again he would stop whatever he was doing and laugh or smile or weep, according to what he saw with his inner sight. Once, standing in the midst of a field of scarlet poppies, he said, "Ah, Bishop Colman has just left Ireland to come to us. He is facing a dreadful storm at Brecken's whirlpool. Even now he raises his hands to heaven to ask that his ship be spared. Let us all join with him in wishing him a safe and speedy passage." And, sure enough, in a matter of days the good Colman arrived and told of his journey, and it was just as Columba had said.

Another time he was with King Aidan of the Southern Cruitne, and the king asked him which of his three eldest sons would rule after him. "None of them," said Columba, "for all three shall be killed in battle. Rather it is one of your younger sons who shall follow you." Then he bade the king call the youths to come to him. And Columba said, "Whichever one of them comes to me and lays his head upon my breast, he shall be king after you." And when the three youths entered the room one of them, who was named Eochid Buide, came and laid his head on Columba's breast. Columba blessed him, and afterward it was just as he had prophesied, for the three elder sons were slain at the battle of Miathi, and of his remaining sons all perished save Eochid, who thus followed his father as king of that place.

As time passed it seemed that Columba could see beyond the bounds of the present with increasing ease, and that all things were transparent to him. Again and again he foretold events that were to come, and things ever fell out as he had said. On one occasion a man named Colca, who would come to hold high office in the ranks of the *Celli Dé,* asked to know the manner of his death. Columba shut his eyes tightly and said, "You shall live a long life, Colca, but when one day you see your cook making merry with his kin of an evening, you shall know that your time is soon to come." And thus it came about, just as Columba had seen.

His prophecies were not always of such high matters. One day as he was sitting in the scriptorium preparing the lettering of a great page, he suddenly stopped and frowned. His attendant, Diormit, seeing this, asked what was amiss. "Truly, it is nothing," replied Columba. "Only that a man who is at present on the other side of the island, but who will join us later, shall knock over my ink pot and cause me to do this page again." And so it came about, for Diormit watched and sure enough a guest came that night who, while looking at the work of the brothers in the scriptorium, spilled ink on the page that Columba himself had been lettering, so that it must be done again.

On another occasion Columba called one of the brothers to him and said, "On the third day from now you must go to the western side of the island, to the shore. There you will find a crane that has journeyed from a distant land, and having suffered much from contrary winds will be utterly spent. Take care of the bird and see that it is fed and looked after." The brother did as he had been told; he found the crane just as Columba had said and cared for it for three days until it was strong enough to continue on its way. When he returned to the foundation Columba smiled upon him and, without waiting for him to relate any of what had occurred, thanked him for caring for "the stranger from a foreign land."

Many said that Columba knew of these things from the Shining One named Axal, who went always with him and with whom he spoke often of deep matters; but others believed that Columba had the ability to look into the inner place and to see what was there, just as the Druids did. Whatever the truth of the matter, throughout his long life Columba made many such prophecies, and many of these were written down and collected in a great book. And in time all of them came to pass as Columba had foretold.

Columba and Mongan

There came a time when Columba could no longer bear to be parted from his own country and he therefore journeyed into Ireland. Once there, he made his way to Carraic Eolaire, on the banks of Loch Foyle, which was a solitary spot such as he might use to contemplate and enjoy his homeland in comfort. Less than an hour had he been there when there came toward him across the water a youth of exceeding beauty, who walked on sandals of bronze upon the water as though it were the earth.

"May the gods of worship bless you, Columba," said the youth.

"Who are you that greets me thus?" demanded Columba.

"Mongan mac Fiachna is my name. I am the son of the king of Ulster."

"How is it that you are alone if you are truly a king's son?" asked Columba.

"As to that, you are alone, are you not?" replied the youth. "Be assured that I could have twice ten thousand men at my side in an instant if I so desired."

"Then why have you come here?" said Columba.

"I have heard that you are great in wisdom," said Mongan. "And since I am reckoned wise among my people, I have come to match wits with you."

Columba smiled. "Tell me something of this great knowledge and wisdom that you have," he said.

"Ah," said Mongan, "there is not a creature in all the world, from the smallest gnat to the greatest whale, whose shape I cannot put upon me. Also I have knowledge of the hidden isles to the west, where few have ever been from the world of men."

"Then tell me," said Columba, "who dwells in these hidden isles?"

"A fair company indeed," replied Mongan. "They have upon them the shape of the fairest men and women, and they possess a great many cattle and sheep; the cattle white as foam, save that their ears are red, and the sheep also white, and more of them there are than the stars in the sky."

"This sounds a most wondrous place," replied Columba. "But tell me what knowledge you have of heaven?"

"I know nothing of this place save for rumors," replied Mongan cautiously. "Will you show me something of it?"

"Return here tomorrow and I shall show you indeed," said Columba.

With that the beautiful youth vanished away and Columba fell to contemplation and prayer.

The next day Mongan came once again walking across the waters of the lake.

"Well," he said, "I am come. What wonders will you show me?"

Columba smiled. "Put your head under the corner of my mantle," he said, "and you shall see all that you would see."

Without hesitation Mongan did as he was bidden, and for a time there was silence, save only for the song of birds and the lap of water.

After a time Columba lifted the edge of his cloak, revealing the face of Mongan, whose eyes were closed in sleep. A smile was on his face and when Columba woke him gently he sprang up and said, "I have seen such things as no tongue could ever tell. Truly this heaven of yours is a most wondrous place. And, strangest of all, it is very like the Otherworld to which I have often journeyed. And yet . . ."

"The same, but different?" asked Columba.

Mongan nodded.

"Then here is a mystery we must both contemplate," said Columba. And with that they took leave of each other, and soon after Columba returned to Iona. But he never forgot that meeting by Loch Foyle, and in later years often spoke of the mystery of the place that was akin to heaven.

THE QUEST FOR THE WISDOM OF THE PAST

This was not the only time that Columba encountered the ancient wisdom of Ireland. There was at a certain time a gathering of bards at the court of the king of Connacht. Senchan, the high bard of Erin, was their leader and he demanded the right of all bards to be served and honored by the king on pain of satire—for it is well known that in those times if a bard made a satire of any man or woman living, he or she would suffer greatly because of it. After a time the king grew tired of feeding this company, who numbered more than three hundred men, women, and servants. Therefore he asked them to move on to another place. At this Senchan grew enraged, and he laid a curse upon all of Connacht, that no poem or bardic song should be heard in that court until they had discovered all of the great epic concerning the Cattle Raid of Culaigne, which in that time had been forgotten and had not been recited in Ireland for many years.

The king of Connacht was greatly disturbed by this, for though he loved to hear the entertainments of the bards, in no way did he know how he might discover the lost epic. Then his brother Marban came to him and said, "Go and seek Columba, for there is no wisdom and knowledge that is not known to him."

So the king, hearing that Columba was in Ireland, went and sought him out. When Columba heard of the difficulty the king was suffering, he thought deeply upon the matter and spoke with the Shining One who went with him always. Then he spoke with the king and told him that he would discover the words of the forgotten epic only by going to the tomb of the mighty hero Fergus mac Roich, for whom the raid of which the poem dealt had been carried out, more than a thousand years before.

So it was that Columba and many of his fellows, together with the king of Connacht, went to the place where Fergus was buried, and there Columba and his brethren, many of whom were holy men and leaders in their own right, prayed and meditated for a day and a night. At the end of that time Fergus appeared before them from the Land of Wonder. So mighty and tall was he that he had to bend down and lie full length upon the earth before he could be heard. Then Columba begged him to help the king of Connacht by telling him the story of the Cattle Raid, and because of the love that he felt for his descendants in the land of Ireland, Fergus recited the whole of the epic, which was written down on the hide of a famous dun cow, for which reason ever after this writing was known as *The Book of the Dun Cow,* which may still be read to this day. Then Columba thanked the spirit of Fergus and bade him return to the Land of Wonder. The king in turn thanked Columba and returned with the book to Connacht and summoned Senchan so that he might hear it recited. And when the chief poet did so, he was filled with wonder at the power of Columba.

THE WHITE HORSE

Now Columba had always known when his death would come, and there came a day, when he was advanced in years and worn out with traveling and teaching, that it was time for him to depart this life. So he set forth for one last time to travel across the island and visit with those of his brethren who had established small enclaves of their own. As he went Columba grew tired and sat down by the side of the road to rest. As he remained there a white horse appeared before him and came and laid its head on his feet. Afterward Columba's attendants said that they saw tears gather in its eyes and roll down its cheeks. But Columba stroked its muzzle and bade it not to grieve just as if it had been a man. Soon the beast rose to its feet, but still it stood by, offering to carry the old man on its back. Columba, however, shook his head. "I have walked thus far through the world and I have not much farther to go," he said. "But I thank you nonetheless." At these words the white horse was gone from there as suddenly as it had come, and all marveled thereat, knowing that such a creature was of the Otherworld and reckoned sacred. But Columba merely smiled and said that he had many friends.

DEATH AND THE CALMING OF THE SEA

So at length Columba returned from his circuit of the island. He stood for a time on the hill overlooking the foundation where he had lived and taught for so many years, and raised his hands in blessing. Then he went down to the scriptorium where he had spent many hours and continued working on the page of the Gospels that he had been illuminating. As evening drew in he said, "After this page Baithene must continue the work." Soon after, he laid down his stylus, and with a sigh made his way to his room. When the bell rang for the midnight service Columba arose and made his way to the chapel, and several who saw him said that he was running as though he were a youth of twenty years or less. Once there he fell upon the ground. There his attendant Diormit found him and cradled him in his arms. Columba looked up at the brethren who gathered about him and smiled upon them all. Then he gave up the ghost.

Two days later he was interred with due solemnity in the graveyard close to the monastery, that same graveyard that housed the bones of Odran. It is told that a great storm arose on the day of Columba's death, but that at the moment he was laid to rest, it ceased and the waters became calm again. Many came from all parts of the land to honor his passing. Later on, his body would be removed from its resting place and reinterred in a grave next to those in which his great soul-friends Patrick and Brighid lay. Columba himself had foreseen this, as did others possessed of foresight. The great poet Dallan Foregail, who knew Columba for a friend to all who sought after knowledge, wrote of him later:

> Noble the tide that reached Iona
> For he that shall be twice buried,
> Columba, true and pure,
> Son of the king of Heaven and Earth.
>
> Iona of many saints
> Foundation of Columba the mighty
> Therefrom at length he departed
> To his joyous bright dwelling.
>
> Thus may Columba be remembered!

◫ ◪ ◫

Columba's story is largely concerned with vision and the intermingling of this world with the other. Again and again we read of the saint's ability to foretell the future, as when he prophesies the fate of the king of Southern Cruithnechan's sons, or seems aware of the difficulties being experienced by a visiting bishop at that moment many miles away.

Celtic tradition is full of seers and prophets, and it is very easy to see how the life of Columba has inherited something of the style and content of prophetic abilities of such figures as the Welsh Taliesin and Merlin and the Irish Fionn and Amairgin. In most stories where these figures are present the connection is made between wisdom, knowledge, and vision, all of which Columba manifested in his own life, while in the lore of the Druids we find these gifts divided up into three orders: the bards, who stored up knowledge; the Druids themselves, who taught the knowledge; and the ovates or seers, who journeyed into the inner places of the soul to bring back the accumulated wisdom of the ancestors.

It is not really surprising to find attributed to Columba a huge catalog of prophetic utterances that rival those of Merlin. The only surprising thing is that the subject of these stories is a Christian saint and that there is little emphasis on God as the source of this wisdom. Rather, Columba seems to possess one of the figures generally referred to as "spirit allies" or "inner guides," to which there are many references in Celtic tradition. Such figures are not unlike the invisible friends often described by children. Attributed more often than not to "an overactive imagination," such figures may be very real and may well have provided us with the concept of the guardian angel.

The actual source of Columba's visionary abilities can be traced to two significant points in his life. The first is the appearance of the mysterious being who calls himself Axal, "Helper." He is generally

*supposed to have been an angel, though even Columba's biographers
seem hesitant to say this with absolute certainty. This is the only
example of a Celtic saint whose inner guide is named, though, as we
have seen, many of those who appear in this book had similar inner
helpers to whom they could turn in times of need. Columba seems to
have been particularly sensitive to such inner prompting, and the
examples of his insight and prophetic gifts are cataloged extensively
in all the versions of his life.*

*The second point from which his prophetic skills seem to derive
is the meeting with the mysterious beggar who always comes late.
One text suggests that the visitor was none other than Christ,
though this is probably a late insertion. The truth is that as with
many wise and holy men this is a turning point in Columba's life—
and as with so many other such people, once the stranger comes
nothing is ever the same afterward.*

*But the gift is a two-edged sword, for those who have the sight
do not always see what they wish to see, and have no control over
the way they use it. To see terrible things that will happen to others
is no easy matter, and requires sensitive handling. Many who are
offered this gift turn away from it, fearing to see things that they
cannot bear to relate. This is the eternal problem of the seer, and
only time and belief in the essential goodness of the gift can bring
them to a full understanding of it. Used wisely it can heal and
redirect us on our spiritual path; used unwisely it can break the
bonds of friendship, love, and trust.*

*Two of the most extraordinary events in Columba's life are the
episode of the burial of Odran and the appeal to the spirit of Fergus*

mac Roich concerning the lost epic poem of the cattle raid. The first episode, which was expunged from most of the versions of his life, has so many echoes of ancient Celtic traditions as to be truly unique. In the first place, there is a marked similarity to the story of Merlin, the famous seer of King Arthur's court, who in an early episode is to be offered as a child sacrifice to enable a building to be completed—a building that, like the one in the story of Columba, falls down mysteriously every night. Merlin avoids this fate by giving vent to prophetic utterance, rather as Odran does. However, while Merlin's prophecies are gathered and recorded, Odran's are not. The reason they are not, we are led to understand in the life of Columba, is that Odran's references to heaven being not what we expect might be threatening to the faith of those who expected to go there. In the original version of the story, no sooner has Odran begun to speak than Columba cried, "Earth, earth upon Odran!" causing him to be immured again at once. I have suggested elsewhere that Columba's innate curiosity as a scholar might have led him to listen to more of what Odran had to say (at least in private), as is suggested by his encounter with the mysterious figure of Mongan, who, despite describing himself merely as the king of Ulster's son, is well known in Celtic mythology as an otherworldly personage. The exchange between Mongan and Columba is a testament both to the latter's curiosity and to the evident parallels between the Christian heaven and the Celtic Otherworld, while the placing of Odran in the darkness under the earth is a well-known method of calling forth a vision, as described in more ancient Celtic traditions.

When it comes to the need for information relating to the wisdom of such ancient times, Columba does not hesitate to assemble his followers and to pray over the tomb of the pagan hero Fergus mac Roich, in order to call him back from the Land of Wonder and to take down the information he has to give. The entire book-length poem is dictated to the saint and is written down on parchment made from the skin of his favorite dun cow. This became The Book of the Dun Cow, which still exists today; the poem, known as The Tain, is perhaps the most famous epic text to have come out of the ancient Celtic past.

The point here is not only that the saints asked an older figure for information, but that Columba received it through prayer and vision and recorded it on the skin of cow—recalling an ancient shamanic method of receiving visions by wrapping oneself in the hide of a yellow cow or a sacred bull before "dreaming" the answers to specific questions. Such practices, like so many of those attributed to the Celtic saints, are very closely allied to the worldwide discipline of shamanism. Indeed, as noted elsewhere in this book, the notion that the saints were "Christian shamans" is a very real possibility.

Much of the underlying power of Columba's story comes from a very human need to know something of the future, to peer beyond the veil and catch a glimpse of what will come to pass. The ability to do this comes, not only from a deep awareness of the spiritual worlds, but also from a close observance of and atunement to the rhythms of life itself. Most people will have been aware at some time or other in their life journey of a sense of predestination. This is not to say that our freedom to choose is taken from us, but rather that certain patterns exist that indicate the connectedness of all things.

This idea is inherent in the majority of the lives of the Celtic saints, and like many of their teachings is in part an inheritance of more ancient beliefs. Our own sense of such a relationship with the cosmos may come only in flashes, but it is possible to extend this for longer periods. Those with such abilities are called prophets and visionaries, people who are so deeply connected to the immense mystery of the universe that they can, quite literally, see through it into the future and into other times and places.

Columba's ability to do this was well attested, and our own latent ability to achieve a similar state of being is by no means impossible. Daily meditation on the small and particular connections—which we often call coincidence or syncronicity—between one event and another, can gradually open our awareness to the larger patterns that are wound into and through the shape of our spiritual journey. This kind of awareness, which is akin to the Tibetan notion of "mindfulness," is not something to be feared but rather embraced. It teaches us how to be "daily visionaries," to perceive the patterns that shape our lives and to become aware of the many kinds of reciprocity that are an everyday aspect of living.

❈ ❈ ❈

Meditation Points

- What patterns can you perceive in your daily life? Are there any larger patterns in your life as a whole?

- Consider whether you have ever experienced anything like a flash of future vision. Ask yourself how this might have come about and whether the vision subsequently came true.
- Draw a "map" of your spiritual journey, showing how certain key points are connected. Meditate on this and try to see the "hidden" aspects of which you are currently unaware. .
- Consider any inner connections of which you are aware between your daily life and that of the other world.

◈ ◈ ◈

Columba's Song of His Exile

Swiftly speeds my coracle,
Its stern toward Derry;
Despite deep grief,
I set my face toward Alba.*

My coracle sings to the waves,
Yet my eyes fill with tears;
Though God blows me east,
My heart yearns for the west.

* *Scotland*

Never more shall my eyes
Feast upon Erin's shores;
Never more shall my ears
Hear her children's song.

Hard-hearted folk in Alba
Jealous and harsh,
Their bodies ill-clothed,
Wracked with disease.

In Eire all hearts are soft,
Tempers gentler, kindly;
The women fair and wise,
The men strong and sturdy.

Trees bent double with fruit;
Bushes full of blue sloes,
Plains lush with grass,
Cattle healthy and fat.

Sweet songs the holy brothers sing
And birds chant with them;
The young are courteous,
The old full of wisdom's words.

My heart's full of love
For my glorious land;
If death should take me
I would grieve the most for Erin's fields.

If Alba were all mine,
From the center to the shore,
I would gladly exchange it
For a field in Durrow or Derry.

Westward take my blessing,
To Eire let my love fly home;
Yet carry my hope eastward
To Alba's shining shore.

—*Trans. J. M.*

CHAPTER 5

THE FRIEND OF ANGELS

SENAN OF SCATTERY

⊠ ⊠ ⊠

Excellent moon, brilliant as the day!
Above the plain he illumines
The tribes of Ireland;
With his many-ranked followers
He sailed through the high heavens.

—Amra Senain

*Like Berach (chapter 10), Senan is a saint about whom little is
known with certainty. His name means "Old Bright One," which
has led to a suggestion that he might have inherited something of the
nature and qualities of an old lunar deity. The Amra Senain, a
poem attributed to the poet Dallan Forgail, compares him to the
moon, his followers to stars, and his work to a river flowing through
Ireland. His name appears in several of the oldest genealogies and he
seems to have been a nobleman, despite the fact that the life refers to
him as the son of a farmer. Born near Kilrush in County Clare, he
studied first with Cassidan at Irrus, then with the famous Nótal at
Kilkenny. He is credited with founding several monastic settlements,
including one at Inniscarra near Cork and others at Inis Mor,
Mutton Island, and Scattery Island, of which the last-named was*

probably the most famous. Ruins can still be see there today,
although they are probably later than the sixth century, when Senan
was active. His bell (actually a small reliquary) is to be found in the
museum of the Royal Irish Academy.

Senan's life paints a picture of a somewhat reluctant leader,
who nonetheless was possessed of considerable powers—including
the bringing back to life of a chieftain's son and the banishment of a
monster inhabiting the islands where he wished to build. He seems
to have been constantly befriended by angels, as witness the episode
of the mysterious helper at the mill (see below) and the advice he
seems able to claim at almost any time. He stood always on the edge
of the spirit realm, moving easily between states of being that
ranged from the heights of spiritual insight to the daily work of
herding cattle and milling corn. Where these two worlds mingled,
the wonder, and the miracles, took place.

◌ ◌ ◌

PATRICK'S PROMISE

One time when Patrick was in Domnach Mor, a deputation
came from the people of Corco-Baiscinn to ask that he visit
them and give them the gift of blessing. And Patrick, whose
great strength was waning at that time, told them that he was
too weary to travel to Corco-Baiscinn, which lay across a wide
expanse of sea from Domnach Mor. The next day they
returned and again begged him to accompany them. But
Patrick would not go, for he had looked into the innermost

place of his soul and seen that another would come who would do that work of blessing for him. First he said to them, "Is your land visible from any part of this land?"

"Indeed it is," said they. "From the hill named Findine you may see part of our land."

"Then let us go there," said Patrick.

So they went to the hill of Findine and from there Patrick blessed the land of the Corco-Baiscinn with increase and well-being throughout the times to come. And he said to them, "There is no need for me to go to your land. For there is even now a child in the womb of a woman of your people that shall do my work for me and bring blessing upon all who seek it and honor to you all."

At this the people of Corco-Baiscinn were amazed, and they were content with what they had been told. Then Patrick pointed to an island that lay in the sea between the two lands. "What place is that?" he asked.

"That is the island of Inis Cathaig," said they.

"Who dwells there?" asked Patrick.

"No one," said they, "for it is inhabited by a monster, which allows no man to come ashore and live."

"This creature does but the work of God," said Patrick, "for it maintains the island that shall one day become a center of wisdom. And the child of whom I have spoken shall come there and build a great foundation and rule over it."

Then he blessed them all again and sent them on their way.

First Wonders

Not long after this there was a great assembly and feasting among the people of Corco-Baiscinn, and among those gathered were a farmer named Gerrgenn and his wife, Coimgell. When they came into the hall a certain Druid, who was greatly respected, rose to his feet and honored these two. Everyone there was greatly astonished at this, for though the couple were well enough liked they were not greatly born or rich. But when they asked the Druid why he honored them, he said, "It is not the man or the woman I honor but the child in the woman's womb. For a vision has told me that he shall be called great and wise and that his coming has been foretold." Then the people remembered Patrick's words and marveled greatly thereat.

Soon after, Coimgell gave birth to a son whom they named Senan, which means "the Old Bright One" in the ancient tongue of Ireland. A strange name many thought this to be, but there were others who murmured that this was not the first time that the soul within the child had walked on the earth. The woman was alone when the pains of birth came upon her, walking in the garden. But it is said that one of the Shining Ones attended upon her and eased her pain. And it is told also that the rowan stake that she held in her hands while giving birth took root and burst into flower. Some say that it may still be seen there, in the place called Magh Lacha.

Not long after the birth of her son, Coimgell went to the well to fetch water, carrying the child with her at her bosom.

Near the well grew a bush filled with ripe blackberries, and there the woman tarried for a while, stripping the fruit from a branch. After a time she heard the voice of the child speaking within her mind: "This is rich fruit, Mother, but there is a richer kind that grows on the borderlands of the spirit." Then she knew indeed that Patrick's words of a wondrous child referred to her own son.

The Fire That Did Not Burn

When Senan was but a youth the Corco-Baiscinn went raiding into the lands of Corcomumruad. Senan was forced to go with them according to the laws of the time, but he had no heart in him to join in the battle or follow the warrior's way. Therefore as the host of the Corco-Baiscinn set forth to ravage the land of their weaker neighbors, Senan went into a barn and lay down to sleep. All around on every side the land was ravaged, but the barn was spared, being somehow unseen by the host. Thus when the warriors returned to their own land they left Senan behind, still sleeping. When the folk of Corcomumruad returned to their burned and blighted homes they found the barn standing, though it seemed to them that flames encircled it and rose above its roof without consuming so much as a single plank of wood or blade of corn.

In time the flames, if such they were, receded and the people were able to enter the barn. There they found Senan sleeping and would have slain him. But something held their hands and instead they awoke him and asked whence he came. In shame Senan confessed that he had come with the host of Corco-Baiscinn, but that he had taken no part in the ravaging. Then some were mindful to kill Senan outright, but others pointed out that not only had the barn been saved by his presence, but the land in the immediate area had also escaped the ravages of the host, while others spoke of the strange fire that burned without consuming. So in the end Senan's life was spared and he returned home unscathed.

THE ROAD OF THE OXEN

One day Senan was herding his father's oxen. He was to drive them from Irrus where they were gathered to Magh Lacha, and between those places there was an arm of the sea that rose in tumult at certain tides. When Senan arrived at the crossing place the waters were already high and darkness beginning to fall. Senan went to the fortress of Mechair, which overlooked the estuary, and begged for shelter for himself and the oxen. But Mechair was away and his servants would not admit anyone. So Senan went back to the edge of the sea and stood there for a long time while the cold bit deeper into his bones.

Then he said, "Enough is enough. I am done with this work." And he raised his hand over the water, which retreated before him and gave way so that he might drive the oxen across in safety. So then Senan went home and told his father that he intended to go to study with the wise and holy teacher Nótal at his school in Cell Manach in the district of Ossory.

Next day Senan set out for Cell Manach and, arriving there, was made welcome. He discovered that his first task was herding the cattle belonging to the foundation, and this he ruefully accepted. But when it came to the time when he must separate the calves from the cattle he found that whenever he set the calves upon one side the cows would at once go there, and when he drove the cows away the calves followed them. In exasperation Senan drew a line in the earth and blessed it, and thereafter the cows and calves went on either side of the line and made no move to cross it. When he saw this Nótal smiled and remembered Patrick's words concerning Senan and knew that a rare, wondrous being had entered the fold of his flock.

THE WONDROUS MILLER

Another of Senan's tasks was to mill corn for the household, and this he loved to do. But one time there was widespread famine in the area and two robbers were abroad who sought to steal anything they could and sell it for profit. Hearing that the mill of Cell Manach was still active and had grain to spare, they went there at night, expecting to find only a lone man whom they could easily overpower. When they looked through a crack in the door, however, they saw two people, one operating the mill while the other read from a book.

The two men thought about this and decided to wait until morning. For, said they, surely one of these men will come forth and go to his home, and when he does so we can ambush him and take the corn he has ground. So they watched all night, and when they looked through the crack in the wall they saw that one of the two men had fallen asleep, but the other toiled on ceaselessly until morning.

When day broke the youth who had been reading came forth with a bag of grain over his shoulder. The two men sprang out and looked into the mill, which was empty. "Where is the fellow who was helping you all last night?" they demanded.

Senan, for it was he indeed, looked at them and smiled. "There was no man there but myself," he answered.

"But we saw another," the robbers said.

"I said no *man*," replied Senan, still smiling. For a moment the two felt the presence of another just behind the youth, and such wonder overcame them that they cast themselves at his feet and begged his forgiveness and blessing. Later they became Senan's devoted followers when he gathered others about him to hear his teachings and learn from his shining example. It was they who told this story long after, and all knew then that it was one of the Shining Ones who had helped Senan in the mill, for others afterward spoke of the youth who worked alone and yet produced enough for two men.

The Chieftain's Son

One time Senan and Nótal went together on a journey to the place known as Cell Mor Arad Tire. When they arrived they found a gathering of people crying aloud with sorrow for the death of their chieftain's son. When they saw the two holy men they rushed toward them, and one, who was the mother of the dead child, fell to her knees and begged them to bring her son back to life. "Only God may do that," said Nótal sadly.

"My child never harmed anyone," cried the woman. "For the sake of his goodness and the goodness of the God you serve, I ask that you bring him back to me!"

Then Nótal looked into the inner place where all visions are found and said, "Bring the child here." When the woman did so, Nótal told her to give him into the arms of Senan. He, with fear in his eyes, cried that his teacher was wrong to ask this of him. But Nótal only said: "It is given to you to do this."

So Senan took the body of the child in his arms and rocked him back and forth for a time and prayed and went inward into the secret place of his soul. Presently the boy was heard to speak, and Senan, with tears in his eyes, gave him back to his mother. Then all there marveled at the miracle, and many wished then and there to follow Senan. But Nótal told them they must wait a while yet, but to come to Cell Manach a year from then. To Senan he said, "Now are the blessed Patrick's words fulfilled. Soon it will be time for you to leave my house and go forth on your own." But Senan was not happy at these words and sought always to cling to the place where his teacher dwelled.

The Way to Monster Island

After the miracle of the chieftain's son, the name of Senan became widely known in Ireland and people flocked to see him. Once again Nótal spoke to him of departure, and of setting up his own foundation. Senan replied, in some anguish, "Dear father, it is not my wish to do this! I am not yet ready to leave you." But Nótal pressed him until at last Senan agreed and prepared to go forth. Yet still he hesitated, asking where he should go. "That is already chosen for you," replied Nótal. "Nor shall I advise you, for the way that you go shall be the way the spirit guides you."

So at last Senan set forth and followed the wandering way for a time, always finding a welcome in the hearts and homes of the places he visited. In time he came to Ferns and there remained in the company of Maedoc for a time, declaring him to be his *anam chara*, his soul-friend in matters of the spirit.

So a year went by and still Senan made no move to set up his own foundation. From Ferns he went to Wales and met with the great David, but the new year found him once again in Ireland, this time settling for a brief time on the island of Inis Cara, where a number of people came to join him. At last, as he lay awake one night, one of the Shining Ones appeared before him, the same that had helped him long since in the milling of corn. The bright being spoke to him and asked why he had not yet settled in a place where all who sought him could come. "I do not know where to go," cried Senan in anguish. "Whatever place my steps are led seems never to satisfy me."

"Come," replied the Shining One, and he lifted up Senan and flew with him to the island named Inis Cathaig, or "Scattery" in the common tongue. There they settled upon a height that is still known as Arn na n-Aingel, "the Height of the Angel," and Senan, whose eyes had been tightly closed from terror of the flight, opened them again and looked around him.

The island seemed a very fair place, but not a single homestead was there upon it.

"Why is this place deserted?" asked Senan. "It seems to be a perfect place to build and make a life."

"The reason is coming closer even now," replied the Shining One. Then Senan looked where he indicated and saw coming toward them the most terrible monster. Its body, black and as large and long as a hillside, ended in a tail that was like that of a whale. A horse's mane it had, and a maw filled with cruel teeth, and iron claws that struck sparks from the rocks as it walked. Its eyes gleamed red and were filled with savage anger. A great heat came from it and a stink of corruption.

When he saw the monster Senan was fearful, but he felt the presence of the Shining One and raised his hand against the beast. It stopped and regarded him with fury and a degree of puzzlement. Then Senan spoke loudly and clearly. "I bid you depart this place," he said, "and trouble this land no more!" He hesitated. "Go to . . . Dubhloch in Slieve Collain, for that is a place where men do not go and where you shall cause no harm."

For a moment it seemed as though the monster would engulf Senan. But at last it turned away from the power it felt within him and dragged its huge bulk into the sea (it is said that the water boiled from the heat of its passing) and so to the farther shore. From there it went into the lake at Sleive Collain as Senan had commanded, and to this day it has been seen no more.

When it was gone from sight Senan walked around the whole island, blessing every place and hallowing it from the dark influence of the creature. "Here then I shall make my home," he said when he had done, and the Shining One smiled and was gone.

SENAN AND THE DRUID

So Senan began to build on the island of Scattery, and people came from afar to hear him teach and to travel with him on his voyage of the spirit. But when news of this came to the ears of Mac Tail, the king of the area, he was angered beyond measure. "Who has dared to enter my lands and settle there without permission!" he cried. Then he summoned his chief steward, Coel, and sent him to remove Senan and his followers from the island.

The steward went to the island and demanded that Senan leave at once. But Senan stood his ground and refused. "For," said he, "it seems to me that your king has no more right to this land than I, seeing as it was I who rid this place of the monster." But Coel would not listen. He ordered the two men who were with him to drag Senan down to the shore and to throw him into the sea. The men, whose names were Coel and Liath, dragged Senan over the rocks until he was bruised and bleeding. But Liath could not bring himself to do further harm to the holy man and refused to help his fellow do the evil deed. The two men argued there on the beach until at last Liath picked up a stone and struck Coel down. Then he helped Senan to rise from the stones.

"You should not have done this deed," said Senan.

"Even though it was to help you?" answered Liath.

Senan shook his head. "Nevertheless, I thank you," he said.

"What will you do now?" asked Liath.

"I shall wait what comes," said Senan, and sat down on the stones.

"Then I shall wait with you," said Liath, and sat down beside him.

When the two men failed to return, the king's steward returned alone to the king and told him that Senan would not go. Mac Tail turned at once to his Druid and demanded what could be done.

"I shall take a charm to him and he shall either die or leave the island," said the Druid.

The king was well pleased at this and the Druid set off at once. When he came to the island he found Senan waiting for him.

"Leave this place," said the Druid.

"I shall not," answered Senan.

"Then I shall make a spell against you."

Senan answered with a charm of his own:

I shall resist your spell.
Disgrace shall be upon you.
You shall be wretched forever.
It is you who shall perish.

"My powers are greater than yours," cried the Druid, though he drew back a step.

"You will do no good," answered Senan. "Whatever you do shall be turned away."

Then the Druid called a darkness over the sun, so that the island was as black as night.

At once Senan called forth the sun again, so that it shone brighter than before.

The Druid responded with thunder and lightning, which shook the earth. But this too Senan put away, so that the sun shone and the storm clouds lifted. Then the Druid became enraged. "I shall go from here," he said, "but you shall not see me go. When I return it shall be with such power that you may not withstand it."

"Go then," said Senan, "but you shall have no luck where you are going."

The Druid called up a thick mist in which he wrapped himself as if it were a cloak; then he went away to an island nearby where he began to make mighty spells and call his forces to him. Senan knew all this, and went to the shore and touched the sea with his hand. At once the waters rose up and covered the island where the Druid had gone. He was swept away and drowned for all his magic, while Senan returned to his hut.

Senan and the King

When the king heard what had happened he was more determined than ever to see Senan put forth from his land. He went himself in his finest chariot and with his finest armor and took ship to the island where Senan awaited him.

"So you are the one who has taken my island from me, and who slew my Druid."

"You forget that it was I who caused the monster to depart," said Senan. "While it remained, no man could come here."

"Nevertheless, the land is still mine," declared the king angrily.

"What man may truly say that he owns any part of the land?" answered Senan. "Surely it is for all men."

"Yet you shall go from here," answered the king.

"You have not the power to make me," Senan answered mildly.

"That we shall see!" ranted the king. "I care nothing for you! No more than for a swarthy, hornless sheep!"

With that he set off back to the land where his chariot awaited him. He determined to gather men and return to drive out Senan by force. But as they drove toward the king's palace a black, hornless sheep burst out of the bushes at the roadside and startled the horses. The king was thrown from his chariot, and striking his head on a stone died instantly.

The manner of the king's death was perceived as a sign of Senan's power, and he was henceforward left in peace, the king's relations declaring the island his in perpetuity.

The Drowned Children

After this, people came from far and wide to join Senan. He began to take pupils and they in turn took others. One of Senan's closest followers, Donnan, had as pupils two young boys that he was teaching to read. On a bright day in spring they went down to the seashore to gather seaweed. While

Donnan's attention was elsewhere, the two boys took a small coracle and set out on their own adventure. But the sea rose against them and they were drowned, their bodies washed up like driftwood on the shore.

Donnan's agony was great, as was that of the children's parents, who came to the shore and stood weeping over the bodies, seeming no more than asleep on the warm sands. Then first Donnan, and after the parents, called out to Senan to bring the children back to life as he had done long since with the chieftain's son. Senan stood in meditation for a time, then bade Donnan speak to the children and tell them to rise. Fearfully Donnan did so. At once the children sat up and began to speak. Seeing their parents there, they reproached them.

"It was no good thing to bring us out of the land where we were," they said.

"Why?" said their mother. "Would you rather be in that land than with us?"

"It is the finest place that ever there was," answered the children happily. "Everything is filled with golden light and music and we can play for as long as we wish without ever growing tired. Do not ask us to return to this land."

Then both the parents wept, for they knew they had indeed lost their children. But Senan said to them, "Do not be sorrowful! I promise you that you shall not feel the pain of loss." Then the children lay down again and spoke no more, and Senan and Donnan took them back to Scattery and buried

them there with the consent of their parents, who in truth felt
but little grief through the intercession of Senan.

The Holly Well

Soon after this there was a year of great drought and on the
island there was little or no water. Every day Senan's followers bemoaned the lack, and begged him to perform some miracle or other for them. Senan always hung back from this,
until one evening as he sat alone one of the Shining Ones who
were ever his companions came to him. "Let us go forth and
discover a place where a well may be sunk," said the angel.

So Senan and his companion went to a place near the center of the island where there was a hollow in the earth. "Dig
here," said the Shining One. Senan dug with a branch of holly
that he found lying near by. As he worked the angel cleared
away the earth, the pair laboring side by side in silent companionship.

Soon freshwater began to bubble out of the earth. "This
well shall not run dry while you or your fellows continue to
live here," said the Shining One.

Senan planted his holly staff there in the earth and it at
once took root. Next morning he came with his companions
to draw water and they found beside the new well a fully
grown tree, which seemed as though it had been there always.
Thereafter, as the angel had foretold, the well was always full
of freshwater for the brethren of Senan.

THE COMING OF CANAIR

One day as Senan walked by the shore, deep in meditation, he saw a figure coming toward him across the water that divided the island from the mainland. As the figure came nearer he saw that it was a woman. She stood upon the water as if it were dry land.

"Well, I am here," she said.

"Who are you?" asked Senan in astonishment.

"My name is Canair," said the woman.

Then Senan knew her for one justly famed for her wisdom, who lived in the south of the land, in the territory of the Benntaige.

"You are welcome," said Senan. "Nevertheless, women do not come ashore here."

"I have heard that all are welcome in the houses of the *Celli Dé,*" answered Canair.

"Nevertheless, I bid you to go and seek the fellowship of women," said Senan. "There is a foundation not far from here."

"It is my understanding that women as well as men may enter the Land of Promise," said Canair. "I have come far to meet you," she added, "and to die here. Shall I get what I desire?"

"You are stubborn indeed," said Senan. Then he laughed and bade her come ashore.

"I shall not trouble you for long," said Canair.

With Senan's permission she made herself a hut there close to the shore, and there she lived out her last days, dying shortly after and being buried in the graveyard of Senan's foundation. In that short time she became firm friends with Senan and they spent many hours together. When her death day came, the wise man was sorrowful, though he knew that she would enter the Land of Promise without hindrance, and that in truth he would soon follow her.

The Death of Senan

So the time came when Senan knew that he was destined to pass from this life, and so he went on a last pilgrimage through the lands of Ireland and Britain to greet those whom he called soul-friends for one last time.

For several months he journeyed, then turned for home. Within a few miles of the craft that would take him across to Scattery he passed through the wood of Cell Eochaille. There, as he drew close to a great and ancient thorn tree, he saw a Shining One standing in the road. "It is time, Senan," said the angel gently. At once Senan's face lit up. Turning to his companions, he said, "I must leave you, my friends. See that my body remains here this night, then take me home."

Senan's companions wept at this, but as he lay down beneath the thorn tree they saw a wondrous sight. Senan's body began to glow with golden light, which swiftly spread to the tree until both were bathed in it. All night the glow burned on, until with the dawn it faded and the body of Senan lay cold and still. Sadly his companions carried him back to Scattery and buried him there. Long after it was said that at night a glow issued from the earth at the site of his grave, and that a thorn tree took root and grew there, shading his final resting place.

◘ ◘ ◘

Senan's name is a vital clue to the possible origin of elements in his life story. "The Old Bright One" can refer to either the moon or the sun. An old praise poem, the Amra Senain, *roughly contemporaneous with Senan's actual dates, describes him in metaphors that include "excellent moon brilliant as the day" and "a golden lamp lit by God," and mentions him sailing "around the heavens" with his followers. He may thus indeed be the inheritor of older figures, gods even, who tended the passages of the heavenly bodies as Senan tended the souls of those who followed him.*

But it is as a friend of angels that Senan is best remembered. Again and again we read of him receiving help and instruction from these unearthly companions. And more so than for most of those with whom he shared this gift, we see the Shining Ones helping him in a very direct way, as in the presence that helps him defeat the robbers, or the physical task of digging the well on Scattery.

Despite belief to the contrary, animosity between the saints and the Druids was rare. Generally, they seem to have recognized each other as like-minded seekers of wisdom who just happened to worship different gods (or anyway, gods with different names).

Magical battles like the one recounted above, however, are often found in ancient texts describing Druid fighting Druid. For example, the text known as The Siege of Drom Damhgaire *describes a druid battle between Ciothruadh who served Cormac, king of Tara, and the famous Mogh Ruith, who served king Fiach of Munster, that is strongly reminiscent of Senan's struggle with Mac Tail's Druid.*

Ciothruadh caused springs and streams to dry up in Tara, but Mogh Ruith relieved the drought. Then Ciothruadh decided to use druidic fire against the enemy. He ordered Cormac's men to go and each cut down a quickbeam (mountain ash or rowan) and make a great fire from the resulting wood. If the smoke drifted south, then Cormac would be victorious, but if it came northward, then Munster would overcome him.

Mogh Ruith perceived their purpose and ordered the men of Munster to bring out of the forest a faggot of rowan wood. Then he ordered that king Fiach should himself bring out a special bundle of wood that had grown in the shelter of three things: sheltered from the northeast wind of March, sheltered from the sea winds, and sheltered from the winds of conflagration that were being lit against them. Mogh Ruith's apprentice, Ceannmhair, built up this wood in the shape of a triangle, with seven vents into it. (Ciothruadh's fire was only heaped up roughly, with three vents.) Then Mogh Ruith asked each of the Munster troops to give him a shaving from the handle of his spear, which he then mixed with butter and rolled into a great ball, saying all the while:

I mix a roaring powerful fire;
It will clear the woods; it will blight the grass;
An angry flame of powerful speed;
It will rush up to the skies above;
It will subdue the wrath of all burning wood;
It will break a battle on the clans of Conn.

Then he threw the ball into the fire whence it exploded with
great force. Saying that he was about to bring a rout upon the
enemy, Mogh Ruith told all to stand ready and watch if the fires
blew northward against their foe. Then "he blew his druidical
breath up into the sky, and it immediately became a threatening
black cloud, which came down in a shower of blood upon the plain
before him, and moved onwards from that to Tara, the Druid all the
time pronouncing his rhythmical incantations."

Mogh Ruith asked what effect the flames were having, because
he was blind. It was reported that the fires were chasing over each
other west and north, and that not a tree in mid-Munster was left
standing. When he asked again, the fires had risen up into the sky
like angry warriors. "Then Mogh Ruith called for his dark-gray
hornless bullside and his white speckled bird headpiece and he flew
up into the air to the verge of the fires, and commenced to turn them
northwards. When Cormac's druid, Ciothruadh, saw this, he also
ascended to oppose Mogh Ruith." But Mogh Ruith knocked
Ciothruadh to the ground and turned the fires north, whereupon
Cormac's army retreated, hotly pursued by Mogh Ruith in his
chariot drawn by wild oxen.

This may seem a far cry from the life of Senan, yet we can see a number of parallels between this druidic battle and his own struggle with Mac Tail's Druid. As so often in this collection, we see that the storytellers who wrought the stories of the Celtic saints drew heavily upon the stories of their predecessors. In Senan's tale there is also the mysterious haunted mill in which, even though the account makes it an angel who is the mysterious helper, we can easily see an older story of a mysterious invisible miller who helped an older hero grind his corn.

Throughout Celtic tradition, as elsewhere, mills were considered sacred and full of an ancient potency, and Senan is only one of many of the Celli Dé who are associated with mills and milling. The idea behind this is perhaps one of spiritual refinement. As grain is processed in the mill, so souls are refined in the "mill of God," the experience of the world. The fact that Senan is helped by a Shining One is another way of saying that we also, each one of us, are helped—or can be if we are willing.

From birth to death Senan is accompanied by angels. He lives ever close to the borderlands of the spirit, speaking of it even while still a babe in arms. From there it is possible to see past, present, and future as a whole—something we can learn to do only with difficulty, but which, once achieved, leaves us changed forever. We may not literally believe in angels, but to act "as if" we are aided through our lives by unseen helpers is to bring an extra dimension into our lives in terms of the shamanic teachings that are so much a part of the lives of the Celtic saints. From their concept of invisible companions, co-walkers who attend us through life and aid us at moments of greatest need, to the concept of "guardian angel" is a very small step indeed.

Senan moves through his life with a sturdy sense of destiny. There is a shapeliness to his life that mirrors the lives of all soul-full people. From the beginning he is destined to find his way to Scattery and build there. The monster that prevents anyone going there before, which "does God's work," as Patrick says, reflects the way that we are sometimes prevented from fully appreciating what is in store for us—our vocation is not a territory into which we need to rush at once; it is a guarded territory that awaits a fully committed approach.

Senan's own life reflects this. For a long time he is fearful of committing himself to the role of teacher and wise man for which he was born. We too can be afraid to accept the gifts and blessings that are given to us, and it may take time before we can do so. Yet once we do, we enter ever more fully into life, perceiving the spiritual present in everything—surely one of the greatest gifts we can know.

Not for nothing is Senan described as:

> A glassy well whereby all who entrusted themselves to him were washed by the purity of his teachings . . . a heavenly cloud whereby the earth and the souls of those that followed him were watered by the rain of his virtues . . . a golden lamp lit by God; . . . a precious stone from which the heavenly palace is built upon earth; a pure vessel by which God's wine is dealt out to the people; a great and happy hospitaller of good fortune. . . .
> —Amra Senain

This last metaphor, of the "great and happy hospitaller" who offers spiritual hospitality to all, is perhaps the most fitting for this wise and holy man, whose welcoming of Canair alone sets him apart from many of his fellows; who dwelt on the borders of the spirit and dispensed goodwill and generosity of the soul to all who found their way to him.

⊠ ⊠ ⊠

Meditation Points

- Do you offer hospitality of the spirit to those around you? If not, consider how you might do so.
- Are you ever aware of angels watching over your life? How might they seem to you if you were to describe them?
- Do you ever cross into the borderlands of the spirit? If so, what does this feel like?

⊠ ⊠ ⊠

Amra Senain
(Dallan in his Blindness)

Bright-eyed Senan,
Swift-flowing dispenser of virtue;
Singular master; wonder-bringer;

Protector of secret wisdom;
Vessel foaming forth words forever;
Who gives bountiful rewards,
Whose treasures are brighter than gold—
May he, the grandson of Dubthach,
Many-branched scion of saviors,
Save me, my sight, and my soul.
May my darkness be broken wide,
May I see again, discover words
Otherwise lost forever.

Idle prisoner of my loss,
I find my way by pronouncing
Senan's name alone. Before:
My verse, eclipsed, my voice
Silenced; after: fogs dispersed,
My words in blossom.
May he save me,
The Old Bright One,
Who watches the heavens,
Ageless and eternal,
Filling the rivers
With bounty of stars.

—*Attributed to Dallan Foregail; version by J. M.*

CHAPTER 6

GIVER OF ALL GIFTS

MOCHUDA OF RAHEN

◉ ◉ ◉

A great household could not be better
Than my oratory in Tuain Inbir.
The stars are familiar to me there,
The sun and moon
In their usual places. . . .

—Anon., ninth century; trans. J. M.

Mochuda, or Catharch as he is sometimes called, was born at Castlemain, County Kerry, about A.D. 570. Adopted by Bishop Catharch the Elder, whose name he may possibly have taken later on, he chose a hermit existence at Kiltulagh before establishing a community at Rahen in Offaly about 595. He was for a time apprenticed to the great teacher Comgall at Bangor. He wrote a verse Rule, which is still extant and which he seems to have received from an angel. In 635 he was expelled from Rahen by Blathnat, the local ruler. He led his community to the banks of the Blackwater and laid the foundations of a great monastic settlement at Lismore, where he is still regarded as the tutelary bishop. That he was not always popular is suggested by the story of the two British monks who tried to murder him in the belief that they should have a new leader, but on the whole he seems to have been a mostly saintly man who could refuse no request, and who gave unstintingly of his remarkable gifts. In the life he comes across as a determined man who went out of his way to deny no one and whose attunement with the natural world produced some astonishing miracles. The story of the rivalry between his foundation and those of surrounding areas rings true historically; there was no central organization within the Celtic monastic communities of Ireland, and disputes and rivalry undoubtedly sprang up from time to time. As with so many of the life stories of the Celtic saints, there are distinct signs of borrowing from older sources, as in the story of the giant Constantine, whose exploits equal those of many an ancient hero.

❈ ❈ ❈

The Blessing of the King

Two prophecies concerning the coming of Mochuda are recorded. A Shining One spoke to Comgall of Bangor, telling him that a child would be born to his race that would have a great future, and with whom he would spend a year of his life. On another occasion Brendan heard of a child who would be named Catharch. Neither knew when or where this would come to pass.

Now it happened that there was an assembly of the tribe of Fergus mac Roich in Ciarraige Luchra, and to this went Figenius, who was a direct descendent of Fergus, together with his wife, Med. The woman was with child at that time, and that night, as the tribespeople gathered in the great hall, a globe of fire was seen by all to descend upon her and hover above her head. On all sides there was great astonishment, and the Druids proclaimed that a great one was about to be born.

Soon after, Med gave birth to a son, who was named Catharch, which is to say "Dear One." From the start he was gifted with great gentleness and sweetness, so that everyone loved him. When he was old enough he was taken to an aged bishop who bore the same name, and this good man took him into his house for fostering. "This child is my portion of goodness," the old man announced, and thus the boy became known as Mochuda because in Irish "my portion" is written *mo chudid*. When word of this birth came to Brendan he knew that the prophecy was come to pass, and he wrote and told Comgall of the event.

Mochuda spent much of his childhood employed in herding swine, along with the other children of his village. One day all the herdsmen went to the royal fort and Mochuda went with them. Somehow it came to pass that the king noticed the boy and began to take an especial interest in him. The queen, when she saw this, asked her husband what it was about the herd boy that fascinated him. "Can you not see?" the king answered in awe. "There is a crown about his head and a pillar of light that reaches up to the sky above him. Mark my words, this is a child of wonder that is among us."

Then the king called Mochuda to him and said, "You have the right to bear arms as did your father. I will give you the best weapons and honors ever given to any man if you remain here and become part of my war-band."

But Mochuda shook his head. "You are generous, my lord, but I prefer the open land and the company of birds and beasts. Nor shall I raise my hand against another in anger or war."

The king was impressed even more by the youth's words, and sorry indeed to see him go. But "if it is your wish," he said. Then Mochuda surprised everyone by taking the king's hand in his and touching him on either shoulder, knee, and foot.

"Why do you do this?" demanded the king.

"Any limb that I have touched this day shall never be hurt in battle nor suffer disease," said Mochuda dreamily, as though he spoke from another place. The king and all those present looked with awe upon the boy, and many now saw the light that was about him in those moments.

THE WONDROUS APPLE TREE

After this, word of Mochuda's gifts spread, and people came to see and hear him. But Mochuda became restless and set forth on a wandering way for a time. First he went to Comgall, who told him of the prophecy he had had years before; then he went to visit Ciaran, who told him that one of the Shining Ones had spoken with him but three nights before and told of his future. Eagerly Mochuda asked what had been said, and Ciaran revealed that there was a place in the heart of Ireland named Rahen that was destined to belong to Mochuda. "There you shall remain for twenty years until you are expelled. Then you shall build a foundation at Lismore and there live out your days."

When he heard this, Mochuda went aside into the wilderness to be alone and to consider these things. There, as he sat in contemplation, came a man named Magus.

"You are the one they call Mochuda?" he asked.

"I am," replied Mochuda.

"I hear you can perform miracles," said Magus.

"It is not I who do them," said Mochuda.

"Nevertheless," said Magus, "I would see some of your wonders."

Magus pointed to an apple tree that stood nearby. "There should be leaves on that tree."

At once the tree was thick with leaves.

"It would be even better if it had blossoms upon it," said Magus.

Mochuda looked at the tree and blossoms sprang out upon it.

"Ha!" said Magus. "What use is a tree without fruit."

Mochuda stirred slightly and the tree became laden with apples.

"They are not very ripe," said Magus.

At once the apples turned red and gold and fell in a shower around the tree.

Magus picked up an apple and looked at it. Then he took a bite and at once spat it out. "There is no point in having a beautiful fruit if it's sour," he said scornfully.

With a sigh Mochuda blessed the apples and at once they possessed all the sweetness of honey.

"That is better!" cried Magus, and ate several of the apples.

Then a strange look came over his face, and stretching forth his hands he cried out in terror that he was blind.

Mochuda took his hands and placed them upon the man's eyes, and with that he could see again. Now he fell down at Mochuda's feet and begged forgiveness for his doubts and foolishness. Mochuda raised him up and embraced him, and after that it was said that wherever Mochuda went, there Magus went also.

THE JOURNEY TO RAHEN

After this Mochuda began his journey toward Rahen. Along the way he met many people who begged him for help, and always he did what he could for them. In one place he healed a madman, in another raised a dead child to life; in yet another he gave back speech and hearing to one who had been stricken deaf and dumb. Elsewhere he healed a leper. Wherever he went it was said that he would refuse no one anything if it were possible—and many things were possible to Mochuda that another might not have done.

One day when they were near the ford of Owenmore in Munster, Mochuda found an apple floating in the water and picked it up. They went on their way for a time after that, until they were in the country of the king of Formoy. Now it happened that the king had a daughter who was paralyzed in one arm, and when he heard that Mochuda was coming that way he went and begged him to perform a wonder and heal his daughter. When Mochuda saw the girl he took the apple out of his robe and offered it to her. The girl stretched out her left arm to take it. "No," said Mochuda, "stretch out your other arm." Wondering, the girl obeyed, and for the first time in her life she was able to move her right arm and take the apple. The king gave thanks and offered lands to Mochuda, but he would not be turned aside, for Rahen had been set aside for him and he would go nowhere else.

When he was still several days' journey from Rahen, a Shining One came to him and told him that he must go more speedily since the king of that land was dying and only Mochuda might heal him.

"It will take me three days at least to get there," said Mochuda.

"Not with my help," answered the Shining One. Then he lifted Mochuda up and flew with him and set him down closer to the king's hall. Mochuda was able to save the king's life that night, and as a reward he had permission to build at Rahen.

Constantine the Giant

First among those who came to offer help in the work of building was a man named Constantine the Pilgrim, a giant of a man who was of royal blood but chose to wander the land helping those who needed it. His strength was great, but his appetite prodigious, and though he did the work of ten men, he seemed to eat the food of twenty. One day he was outside digging a trench and it happened that the rest of the community went to eat but forgot him. When he realized what had happened Constantine flung a shovelful of earth over the roof, so that some of it went in through the openings that had not yet been covered and into the plates and cups of those within. The commotion that ensued brought Mochuda himself to deal with the problem. He found Constantine in the trench, sweat running down his brows. Mochuda smiled at his hardest worker and himself wiped some of the sweat from Constantine's brow. "Your sweat will always heal people from now on," he said. And so it was, for afterward it is said that anyone who touched Constantine when he was working and got some of his sweat upon him, if that person was sick he was at once made better.

Expulsion

So the foundation grew apace, and word of Mochuda's teachings and wondrous acts went out through the land. People began to flock to Rahen, until it was hard to sustain them all. One day a man named Lasianus came to see Mochuda, and secretly brought with him thirty cattle that he intended to offer to the community. But first he wanted to test Mochuda, so he pretended to be unwell, saying that he could drink only milk—this in the knowledge that there were no milking cows at Rahen. Mochuda brought forth a flagon of water, and as he walked spoke words of blessing over it. When he handed it to Lasianus it was filled with milk.

After this many others came with gifts, and soon the foundation was the richest in the neighborhood. Thus the leaders of other, smaller communities began to feel jealousy toward Mochuda, calling him proud and greedy and other unworthy names. Soon a party of these jealous men went before the new king of the area—the old one having died—and petitioned him to expel Mochuda, giving as reason many vile calumnies and lies against him.

The new king, whose name was Blathnat, was inclined to believe the slanderers, and went with his brother Dairmait, who was a king in his own right, to expel Mochuda and his followers from Rahen. When he saw them coming, Mochuda asked Constantine to go forth and meet with them. "Ask them to grant me a year before I must leave," he said.

Constantine went forth with his great club in his hands. When the two kings saw the giant coming, they looked at each other.

"I have come to ask a year's grace for Mochuda," said Constantine mildly.

"It is granted," said Blathnat, and the two kings returned home.

So the year passed, and soon the kings returned, this time with more men.

Again Mochuda asked Constantine to ask for a year, and again he went forth. The kings pretended not to see him, but Constantine went right up to them and said, "This is neither wise nor polite. Once I had as many as seven kings at my command, and more sheep and cattle than all of you. Now I have nothing but the clothes I stand up in and this club. This I do for the love of God and Mochuda. Will you talk with me?"

"We will grant you another year," said the kings, and went their way.

So the time passed, and at the end of that time Blathnat and Dairmait returned for the third time. Once again it was Constantine who met them. This time they decided to be firm with him. "You will get no greeting from us," they said, "unless you and all who dwell here are willing to depart."

Constantine walked up to the two kings and seized them both by the neck, one in either hand. "Unless you grant Mochuda another year's grace you shall be covered in each other's brains," he said gently.

"It is granted," gasped the kings, as best they might.

The Founding of Lismore

Sadly, soon after this, Constantine died. Great was the mourning of all, for he had been much loved. Now, without him to protect them, the community were driven forth, and Mochuda led them along the hot roads of midsummer until they reached the territory of the Deisi. The king of those people, who was named Maelochtraig, gave them permission to stay, for that very day his wife had told him of a vision in which she saw a great flock of birds settling on the land and one, which seemed their leader, on the king's own shoulder. "That will be Mochuda and his people," said the king, and went out to welcome them.

So the community settled there and began to build a great foundation at a place called Lismore, which was indeed the very place where it had been foretold that Mochuda would one day come. There he grew old, and there, one day, as he was sitting in the sun watching his followers struggling to cut a field of corn, Mochuda rose to his feet and said, "Soon I must leave you all, but there is one final gift I may give you. You may have more reapers to help you." Then, it is said, a company of the Shining Ones came among them and cut the corn for them while they marveled.

Soon afterward Mochuda died, and many who witnessed it told how a great company of angels came to meet him, and carried off his soul in a blaze of glorious light. After his death many wonders were performed in his name, and people continued to say that no request made to Mochuda was ever refused, if it were possible.

❂ ❂ ❂

Mochuda was a giver throughout his life. Whenever anyone asked for anything he tried to give it—from the demands of the strange, challenging Magus (clearly either a Druid or a magician) that the apple tree be given blossom, fruit, and flavor; to the multitudinous requests for sight, hearing, speech, cures for leprosy and paralysis, and much more. Of course, all the saints were asked to perform miraculous cures, and most of them did so, but none perhaps as unstintingly as Mochuda.

The most interesting character in the story, however, is Constantine, the giant pilgrim who not only does the work of ten men (and has the appetite to match) but also protects Mochuda and his followers from the incursions of their jealous neighbors and the kings of the area. There is little doubt that Constantine is based on one of the older Celtic heroes—Cuchulainn perhaps, though he is a far less gentle character than Constantine. Or perhaps one of the several figures in Celtic myth who derive from the Greek hero Hercules is the real origin of this wonderful character.

One such candidate in particular leaps to mind: Ogma, to whom is attributed the creation of the mystic Ogam alphabet, a device used by the bards and Druids to pass messages among themselves and to invoke the gods. In one text, this character is referred to as Ogma Cermait (Honey-Mouthed) and Trenfher

(Strong Man, Champion). The Classical author Lucian wrote that he was the Celtic Hercules, and gives a description of a painting that depicts an ancient figure drawing a group of men chained by their ears to his tongue.

Puzzling over this painting, Lucian found a native Celt at his side who was willing to elucidate:

> We Celts do not agree with you Greeks in thinking that Hermes is Eloquence: we identify Hercules with it, because he is far more powerful than Hermes. And don't be surprised that he is represented as an old man, for eloquence . . . is wont to show its full vigor in old age. . . . This being so, if old Hercules here drags men after him who are tethered by the ears to his tongue, don't be surprised at that either: you know the kinship between ears and tongue.
>
> —Lucian Heracles

Ogma's title Trenfher suggests an actual identification with Hercules/Heracles, whereas his Hellenized name means "the Walker," and if we recall that the original meaning of the word pedant is derived from scholar, or "one who walks up and down," we may see how this follows. Constantine, who walks the roads as a pilgrim and seeks to serve others, seems a perfect descendent of Ogma, and offers yet another example of the way in which the writers of the saints' lives drew upon older material.

Mochuda is a giver of all things. His generosity begins with the spirit and extends outward to embrace all his fellow creatures—in which he includes animals and birds, those whose company he *prefers as do so many of his fellows. Drawing strength from the inner world of the Shining Ones, as well as from the natural energy of the land and its inhabitants, he is able to offer the greatest gift of all: unconditional love. This is perhaps the hardest thing we can encompass in our own lives, to give all and ask for nothing in return. Yet, with practice, we can accomplish much, beginning with small gifts of kindness and building slowly, at our own pace, to larger acts of generosity and love. That this is hard for us to do is partly because of the way we live today. We are encouraged to think only of ourselves and nothing more. Yet, if we move beyond the often self-imposed barriers of selfishness and self-centeredness, we will begin slowly to open ourselves to the place where we can serve others also. This is Mochuda's deepest message to us, and one from which we can learn a great deal on our own journey.*

◩ ◪ ◩

Meditation Points

- Do you consider yourself a giver? If not, what would it take to make you into one?
- Do you hold back from giving of yourself, and if so, why?
- What would you consider the greatest gift that you could give another?
- Think of three examples of times when you have received an unqualified gift of the spirit.
- What differences, if any, are there between gifts of the spirit and ordinary gifts?

Mochuda of Rahen

⊞ ⊠ ⊞

The Voyage of Cormac mac Culennan

Shall I choose, O King of the Mysteries,
After delighting in downy pillows and sweet music,
To go upon the rampart of the sea,
Turning away from my native land?

Shall I be poor in battle,
Through the grace of the undying king,
Without honor, lacking my chariot,
Without gold, silver, or horse?

Shall I launch my dark coracle
On the broad and glorious ocean?
Shall I go, O King of Heaven,
Of my own will on the brine?

Whether wide or narrow,
Whether served with hosts or not,
God, will you stand by me
If I go to the angry sea?

—*Anon., eighth century; trans. J. M.*

CHAPTER 7

THE FRIEND OF
THE SPIRIT
DAVID OF WALES

◼ ◼ ◼

The road to old St David's
Is the white road of the blest . . .
When all the wandering roads of Wales
Went winding to the West.

—*A. G. Prys-Jones*, A Song of the Pilgrim Road

Given his popularity and importance as the patron saint of Wales, surprisingly little is known about David. He was born about 520, reputedly the offspring of a casual mating by King Sandde of Ceredigion and Non, who herself went on to become one of the best-loved saints of Wales. He is first mentioned in an eighth-century Irish document known as The Catalogue of the Saints *and again in the slightly later* Irish Martyrologies. *These state that his chief monastic foundation was at Menevia, believed to have been located where the present-day Saint David's Cathedral stands in the city of Cardiff. In fact, he may have begun his career in a monastery at*

Henllan in Dyfed (Pembrokeshire), which he received as a gift from his father. He is also said to have founded a settlement at Glastonbury, one of the many great saints claimed by that center of myth and tradition, and possibly as a result of this he is also said to have been the great-nephew of King Arthur.

David is mentioned in several other lives as a mentor or soul-friend to Maedoc of Ferns, Senan of Scattery, Findbarr of Cork, and Brendan of Clonfert. The picture of monastic life contained in the eleventh-century account of David written by Rhygfarch is believed to be a particularly accurate one, with its emphasis on personal toil in the fields and farms, abstinence from all liquors save water, and the daily round of prayer and contemplation.

In the life David comes across as a strong-willed man dedicated to the work of learning and teaching. The strictness of his regimen—he used often to stand up to his neck in icy water for hours at a time—has led to a belief that he was himself cold and unsympathetic. Nothing seems farther from the truth, however, when one reads the story of his life with its many magical and soul-driven acts, such as the curing of his teacher's fading sight and the wonderful episode in which he enables the visiting Findbarr to cross the ocean on the back of a horse—an account that could have stepped from the pages of a far more ancient tale.

David was known familiarly to the Welsh nation as Dewi, and a pilgrimage to Saint David's—performed twice—was considered equal to a journey to Rome. This practice is still followed today.

Son of the Sea

One night as he lay abed in his palace at Ceredigion in Wales, King Sandde awoke to the sound of a voice speaking in his ear—though he could see no one in the room. "Tomorrow," said the voice, "you shall go hunting. Near the river you will kill a stag, and in that place you shall find three gifts: the stag itself, a fish, and a hive of bees. Send these to the foundation of Maucannus, where they shall be kept for a son that shall issue from you."

The king was fearful at this, but on the morrow he set forth as the voice had instructed him, and sure enough he chased and killed a great stag, and at the spot where it fell next to the bank of a river, he found a fish lying on the bank, while overhead a hive of bees hung buzzing in a tree. Marveling, Sandde commanded his followers to take these three things to the nearby monastery of Maucannus while he himself returned to the palace alone. As the king followed the road close to the sea, he happened to pass a young woman who was so beautiful that he was instantly inflamed with desire for her. There and then, against her will, the king raped her, then went on his way leaving her behind. The girl, whose name was Non, had been a virgin until this time. Knowing that she would be outcast from her village, she went her way alone, wandering the roads of Wales until she found a small sheltered cave on the seashore. Here she made her home and waited the coming of the child that was soon kicking within her.

One day she made her way to a local church where the famous teacher Gildas was speaking to a great gathering of people. As soon as Non entered the church he was unable to speak a word, and by signs indicated that he wanted to be left alone. Everyone went out of the church except Non, who was curious to see what would happen and hid behind a pillar. For a while she watched Gildas struggle to speak. Finally he was able to say, "Someone is hiding here. Come out at once!" Shyly Non emerged and at once the man's tongue was loosed. He asked the girl who she was and had her story from her. "I believe the child that grows within you will be a great teacher," he said, "for in the presence of such a one I am silenced!"

King Sandde meanwhile had learned from his Druids that the child whose coming had been foretold by the mysterious voice would be born to the girl he had taken so casually on the road. Now he set out to seek her, and soon learned of the strange wild girl living in the cave by the sea. It was at this very time that Non felt the onset of her birth pangs. Driven by a need she could not express, the girl left the cave where she had been living and sought the place where her child had been engendered. As she went, the sea rose and the heavens opened and rain deluged the place. Lightning flashed, thunder rolled, hail lashed the earth with whips of ice. Weeping, Non hastened on as best she might until she reached the spot where King Sandde had found her. There, to her wonder, was a meadow where the sun shone, the rain fell not, and the earth seemed as soft to her as a bed. Here she gave birth, grasping a stone that was said to carry the marks of her fingers ever after. And here King Sandde found her, cradling her newborn son to her breast. The king knelt down beside her and begged her forgiveness. "This child is destined for greatness," he said. "If you will let me, I will care both for it and for you."

Non agreed, and returned with the king to Ceredigion. Ever after, it is said, her child, who was given the name of David, loved the sea and went there whenever he could, so that in time to come he was often called "the Son of the Sea."

A Gift of Sight and a Prophecy Fulfilled

Once her child was old enough to be put out to fosterage, Non returned to the place where she had given birth and there set up a small cell in which she lived out her days, becoming known throughout Wales as a wise and holy woman famed for her gifts as a healer—especially of sicknesses suffered by women in childbirth. David was fostered with a wise teacher named Paulinus, in a place called Menevia. There he learned to read and write and began to study the mysteries. It is said that it was at this time that he befriended a dove, which afterward went everywhere with him, sitting on his shoulder, and was even believed by some to teach him the secrets of the world. It was also at this time that he performed his first wonder.

When David had been at Menevia for several years, his teacher, Paulinus, began to suffer with inflammation of the eyes. When this became so bad that he could scarcely see, he called all his pupils to him and asked them to bless his eyes, hoping that they might be healed by the touch of caring hands. When David's turn came he hesitated, and when pressed admitted that in all his time at the school he had never once looked his master in the face. Moved by this show of humility, Paulinus said, "Without looking raise your hand to my eyes. I know they will be healed." David did so, and at once his teacher could see again as well as he ever had.

Not long after this one of the elders from the foundation of Maucannus came and spoke of a dream he had had. In this dream one of the Shining Ones had come to him and shown him three things that had been sent to them years ago by King Sandde. These were: meat from a stag, together with a huge salmon, both miraculously preserved, and a hive of bees that had continued to give great quantities of honey ever since the king's men had brought it there. These, the angel told him, were intended for a youth who even then was a pupil at Paulinus's school.

When he heard this story, the teacher knew at once that the youth must be David, and sent for him. Tears sprang to David's eyes when he learned the story of his father's vision, and it was agreed that he would travel back with the visitor to Maucannus. Once there, after much thought, David prepared a meal with the flesh of the stag and the salmon, cooked in honey from the beehive. This he served up for all who were guests of the foundation, and it was said that never was there such a feast in all that part of the land. Afterward David returned to Menevia, bringing the hive with him. Many saw a change in him, and spoke of a new sense of purpose that he had. Thereafter he loved to keep bees and when he finally ended his wandering days, there were always hives on hand to feed the community.

The Death of Dunawd

Thereafter the fame of David's miraculous gifts began to spread, until his teacher declared that it was time for his pupil to set forth and begin the work of founding schools of his own. Reluctant at first, David set out on a pilgrimage through the land of Britain, visiting many of the foundations already set up by the *Celli Dé*. Yet, though he constantly sought to find a place where he might settle, always one of the Shining Ones would speak to him, telling him that another place awaited him "beyond the next hill or valley." Over a year after leaving Menevia he was close to home again, and there at last the Shining One told him of a place nearby where he was destined to be. A small, sheltered valley, it lay in the shadow of a huge crag named Clegyr Fawr, on which stood a fortress belonging to an Irish freebooter named Boia. The spot to which David was led, which was called Glyn Rhoslyn, had long since been marked out for settlement by Saint Patrick, but the great teacher had been turned away by his own angelic guide, who told him: "This place is destined for another, who shall be led here in time to come and will do great wonders in this spot."

So David and his small band of followers began to work to tame the wild land and make it ready for those who would come. Thus it was that they came to the attention of Boia, who truth to tell cared little for who might settle on his land, so long as they left him in peace. Boia's wife, however, was incensed by the presence of the *Celli Dé* and insisted that her husband go forth and drive them out.

Boia arrived at the small circle of huts where David and his followers were living and demanded that they leave. But David stood his ground, and such were his gentle ways that Boia found himself giving permission for the work to continue, providing that the settlement spread no farther than the valley.

Boia's wife was furious when she heard this, and set about her own plans for driving out David and his slowly growing band. Her first plan was to send all her maids to bathe in the stream near the settlement, hoping that the presence of laughing, naked girls would cause them such embarrassment that they would leave willingly. Indeed, the monks were at first put out by this, but David told them to be patient: "They will soon tire of this sport, and once the weather turns cold, they will stop coming."

And so it was; but Boia's wife did not relent in her animosity toward the *Celli Dé*. Her next plan was both desperate and dark. She sent word to her stepdaughter, who was named Dunawd, to come and visit her, and when the girl came she took her to a lonely spot farther up the valley in search, she said, of hazelnuts. When they had been there for a time the woman lay down, feigning tiredness, and invited Dunawd to lay her head in her lap. Then, as the girl slept, Boia's wife took out a knife and cut her throat, so that her blood flowed into the stream. Then she cut off the girl's hair and made an offering of it to her gods.

Somehow she believed that this terrible act would cause the community to vanish entirely. But when it failed to have any effect, and fearful that the murder of Dunawd would be discovered, the woman crept out of the fortress at night and fled away, never to be seen again. That same night, a rival pirate named Leschi crept up to attack the fort. Finding the gate open, left that way by the fleeing woman, the pirate entered and slew everyone therein, including Boia, who died in his sleep and without even having time to draw his sword.

When David heard of these events great sorrow overcame him. He went to the place where Dunawd had been killed and there blessed the earth. A small spring of clear water began to bubble out of the ground, which thereafter was known for its curative properties.

Honey and Wild Horses

David's small community became famed for its strict regime. David insisted that his followers should be self-sufficient, breaking the land by dragging the plow themselves, milling their own flour, planting and harvesting what they needed to feed themselves and those who came to visit. Their daily routine of prayer and meditation became a model for many who came after them, and the simplicity of their way of life became the fulfillment of all who sought to follow the path of the *Celli Dé*.

David himself remained especially fond of bees, and kept several hives that were the descendants of the one discovered by his father. One day Modomnoc of Leinster came on a visit from Ireland to Menevia. He remained there for some weeks, and spent many hours helping David tend the bees. When it came time for him to depart, a swarm of bees followed him and attached themselves to the prow of his ship.

Not wanting to deprive the community of its precious cargo of honey, Modomnoc walked back to Menevia, with the bees following. When David saw what had happened he laughed: "Evidently my bees like it better where you are going. Let them go and take my blessing with them, that they grow and increase in your land." With that he blessed the bees, and Modomnoc returned with them to his ship. It is said that thereafter the bees of Leinster were more plentiful and gave better honey than in any other part of Ireland. Modomnoc himself said that the community of Menevia was itself like a hive, whose honey was pure wisdom and the wonder of David's inspired teaching.

Many other visitors found their way to the sheltered valley—among them Findbarr of Cork. He remained with David for a month or more, discussing everything from the names and virtues of the stars to the nature of the Shining Ones.

Eventually the time came for Findbarr to return home, but he was prevented from departing by contrary winds that kept his ship penned in the harbor for day on day. Findbarr began to fret about the delay, visualizing all kinds of disputes and quarrels that might have arisen in his absence. Then one morning he came to David and begged a favor of him. "That horse you used to ride everywhere on—do you still have it?"

"Why, yes," answered David, puzzled.

"May I borrow it for a while, and will you give the animal, and myself, your blessing?"

"I will do both, and most willingly," replied David.

Findbarr mounted the horse and rode straight down to the seashore. Here, to the astonishment of everyone, he kept on going into the water, and was last seen riding across the tops of the huge waves as though the sea were a level plain.

With wind and rain lashing him on every side, Findbarr rode on across the ocean toward Ireland. On the way he met with Brendan, who was engaged on his own voyage of wonder, and was at that moment riding the back of the great sea creature Jasconius. There Findbarr paused for a while, and he told Brendan about David. "Truly these are wondrous times," said Brendan, and promised to visit Menevia himself when his voyage was done. Then Findbarr went on his way and soon arrived back in Ireland, having ridden all the way on the back of David's horse. When he told his own companions of his journey they were filled with wonder and thereafter cared for the horse until the day of its death. Afterward it became a say-

ing that as the sea had horses, so had David of Wales his own
wondrous steed.

The Passing of David

For many more years David continued to teach at Menevia,
which expanded to become a settlement of some size. In addition, he set up other foundations of learning and wisdom and
traveled widely throughout the lands of Britain. Once, when
he was copying a page of the Gospels in the scriptorium, the
bell rang to call the community to prayer. David left the page
half done but, when he returned later, found that it had been
completed in letters that blazed with gold. For many years
after, the book was kept hidden at David's bidding, but after
his death it became famed throughout the land, and people
came from great distances to see it. But in time David grew
old, and there came the day when, sitting in his cell, he
received a visit from one of the Shining Ones, who told him
that the time was approaching when he should pass from this
life. David greeted the news with delight and told his followers, who were greatly cast down.

"Do not be sad," David told them. "This is a day I have
longed for all my life."

Thereafter as the day drew near David spent his time
preparing himself for his death. And, none knew how, word of
his imminent passing spread throughout not only Britain but
Ireland also, and people began to come from all over these

lands to pay homage to the holy man. Like bees they gathered to the hive of Menevia, which was made abuzz with the voices of those who wished to see David one final time.

On the fifth day of March he gave one last address to the gathered people, bidding them "Do these little things we have spoken of." Shortly after he became seized with pains and was carried to his cell, where he died that night. Afterward many bore witness to the fact that the building was filled with light and with a singing that could only be that of the Shining Ones themselves, and thereafter many wonders were wrought in the name of David of Wales.

❊ ❊ ❊

In nearly every instance, births of saints are announced or predicted, either by angelic informants or through other signs and wonders—although no other perhaps as dramatically as David's coming, which is foretold by the gifts of a stag, a fish, and a hive of bees. All three were considered sacred among the Celtic peoples—the stag for its strength and otherworldly appearance (Arawn, the lord of the underworld, sometimes rode on a stag); the salmon for its association with the story of Fionn mac Cumhail, who ate of such a sacred fish and imbibed wisdom with it; bees because they were considered to be oracular creatures and guardians of the land's bounty. Singly these images might mean little; collectively they say very clearly that a child of wonder is coming.

This, together with the dramatic nature of his conception (though he is not alone among the saints in being born illegitimate;

Kentigern is another), singles out David as an important figure, whose credentials would have been recognized by both pagans and Christians—a useful attribute in a time when the two spiritualities often clashed with each other.

The story of the sacrifice of the girl Dunawd is a further example of the way in which those who forged the lives of the saints strove to echo earlier tales, shaping them to their own needs while remaining true to the original. At one time the slaying of the girl might well have taken place in a ritual setting. The use of it here as a story device is further extended by the aftermath: the evil woman vanishes, her husband is slain, and a spring of healing water rises where the girl died. There is even some evidence that Dunawd may have been revered as a saintly person herself and that she was the center of a minor cult in the area where these events were believed to have taken place.

There is also the matter of David's wondrous horse, which is able to cross the ocean as though it were on dry land. Among the Celtic deities, Manannan mac Lir, the god of the sea, possessed such a horse, called Aenbarr; no rider was ever killed while on its back. Many of those listening to the story of the saint would have recalled this miraculous beast and its owner.

David himself is portrayed as a late starter, full of modesty and gentleness. The episode in which he restores the failing sight of his teacher is typical of the shyness that he strove to hide in later life but perhaps never completely overcame. His dying words, in which he bids his followers remember the "little things" that he had taught them, ring true. David's teaching, like the Rule that he established in all his monastic foundations, was simple in the extreme, and did indeed serve as a kind of exemplar to other communities.

In his desire to serve God as directly as possible, David reduced his approach to the utmost simplicity: daily prayer, meditation, and a strict honoring of the canonical hours. Simple food, simple words, simple truths. Yet how profound these could be! As with all the Celtic saints, David lived close to the natural world, emphasizing the need to till the soil with his own hands, to be self-sufficient as far as was possible. In our own time we have only recently begun to appreciate the need to live in this way, and though it may be true that we can probably never all be self-sufficient in this way, the honoring of the earth is more important today than ever before. The effect of this is to bring us into the curve of David's own truth and practice.

As well as being a child of the sea, David was known as "the Waterman," in part at least because of his refusal to drink anything other than water. Aside from this there is a deeper meaning to this name. David can also be seen as one who ferries the souls of the living across the water of life and into the service of the Spirit, who brings those who follow his way into a quieter harbor where the spirit can grow and flourish unimpeded by the speed and complexity of life. Water cleanses all things, and quenches our deepest thirst. At certain times in our lives, if we are fortunate, and quiet enough, we are able to drink from the sacred well whose waters can spiritually refresh us.

MEDITATION POINTS

- Ask yourself how you could live a simpler life within the world.
- How would the world seem to you if everyone were able to live more simply?
- What things can you personally imagine doing without to make your life more in keeping with the simplicity of David's teaching?

⊞ ⊞ ⊞

A Medieval Sequence of Saint David
David, splendid star,
Shines over Britain;
His sacred converse
Adorns Menevia.

Proclaimed by angels;
by stag, honey,
fish and flowing water,
Signs that showed
His imminent nascence.

Champion of Britain,
Teacher to the Cymry,
Seeking sanctuary

In the wild vale's
Sheltered places.

Sea's Son named;
Healer, teacher,
Spiritual friend;
Acclaimed by all,
His name remembered
Ever after.

—Fifteenth-century Hereford missal; version by J. M.

CHAPTER 8

A Vision of Trees

Ciaran of Clonmacnoise

❖ ❖ ❖

Down the five roads of Erin:
By rath and bog they passed:
Ciaran of Clear was the first,
But who shall be the last.

—Patricia Lynch, Ciaran

Ciaran of Clonmacnoise came of a line of bards and poets, which may account for his love of learning and his close relationship with the natural world—especially trees, for which he seems to have had a more than usual love. He was born in the ancient kingdom of Mide (Meath) about A.D. 512, the son of a chariot maker, and seems to have demonstrated remarkable qualities from birth. While still a youth he went to study at the school of another remarkable teacher, Finnian of Clonard. This man, who is remembered as a poet as well as a saint, taught twelve of the most important Celtic monastic leaders, known as "the Twelve Apostles of Ireland," of whom Ciaran was one.

Ciaran himself had a wide circle of soul-friends, including Columbcille (Columba), Enda of the Aran Islands, and Kevin of Glendalough. His friendship with the warrior Diarmit son of

Cerball, who is a historical figure, is also recorded. A poem included in the life of the saint predicts the future of Diarmait:

> I will bear witness truly
> Though your company be only one,
> You shall be a great and dignified king
> Of Ireland by this hour tomorrow. . . .
>
> Without rout or slaughter
> You shall take Usnach;
> Diarmit, the distinguished,
> Gave a hundred churches to Ciaran.

With the new king's blessing, Ciaran founded a great community at Clonmacnoise (Cluain Mocca Nois) toward the end of A.D. 544, but died less than a year later at age thirty-three, probably of the yellow plague that also carried off Finnian. The ruins of the monastery may still be seen, on the banks of the river Shannon, to this day.

❁ ❁ ❁

First Wonders

Ciaran was born at Rath Cremthainn in the province of Connaught after his parents, Beoit and Darerca, fled from the heavy tribute laid upon them by the king of Ui Neill. Beoit was a carpenter and a chariot maker, and the king of Connaught was glad to make him welcome and set him to work. But when the king's Druid, Lugbrann, saw Beoit and Darerca coming toward the fort in a chariot he laughed aloud.

"Why do you laugh?" asked the king.

"I laugh," said Lugbrann, "because of what I see coming in that chariot."

"I see only the carpenter and his wife," said the king.

"There is another," answered Lugbrann. "The woman bears a child in her womb that shall be as great a man as any now living in Ireland. He shall be a child of the trees, and he shall give a gift to your son." But more than that he would not say.

In time Darerca gave birth, and her son was named Ciaran. He grew to be a cheerful, kindly youth, who was forever running off into the woods. Indeed, he loved nature so much that it was often said of him that he knew the nature of every plant and herb and tree in all of Ireland.

One day when Ciaran was twelve years old, a horse belonging to Oengus, the king's son, died. The youth was heartbroken, for he had loved the steed better than anything else in the world, and he knelt by its side and wept long and hard. When Ciaran saw this his own heart filled with sorrow, and he went up to the king's son and bade him ease his sorrow. "I will pray to the great God who made the world that he give you back your horse."

Oengus stared in wonder as Ciaran took some water and blessed it and then scattered some over the body of the horse. At once the beast began to breathe again, and rose and stood again upon its legs. Oengus was so happy that he could not speak, and thereafter he and Ciaran became close friends, despite their different stations. Thus was the Druid Lugbrann's prophecy fulfilled, and many years after, when Ciaran founded his first community of monks, Oengus gave him lands, which became known as Tir na Gabra, "the Land of the Steed."

On another occasion, soon after this, Ciaran's mother scolded him for forgetting to bring honey from the hives in the village. At once Ciaran took a jar and went outside to the well that stood near his house. He filled the jar with water and blessed it. Then he took it to his mother and she found that it was filled with the purest honey.

At another time his father sent Ciaran to a neighboring king named Furban with a cauldron that he had ordered. But on the way Ciaran met with a group of poor folk who had nothing in which to cook their meager fare, and he gave the vessel to them. When King Furban heard this he ordered Ciaran put to work grinding corn with a quern until he had paid off the debt. But when Ciaran stood by the quern it turned of its own accord, so that everyone was astonished and afraid. Next day a smith came from the province of Munster with a gift of three cauldrons for the king. Ciaran was set free at once, and returned home.

After this, word began to spread of Ciaran's miraculous powers. Many said that he must be destined to follow the way of the *peregrini*, the wandering wise-folk who lived close to God in the wilds. And so it was decided that he should go to the school of Finnian at Clonard to learn wisdom and find his way.

Ciaran set out on a bright May morning just after his thirteenth birthday. He took with him a cow, whose milk would pay for his tuition. And indeed, after he blessed it, so much milk did it give that neither Ciaran nor his fellow students ever wanted for sustenance while he was at Clonard.

Miracles at Clonard

For the next few years Ciaran remained at the school, learning everything the wise Finnian could teach. But always there were wonders, marvelous and miraculous events that followed Ciaran wherever he was.

Whenever he could Ciaran would spend his time outside. He liked to read in the open air, sitting in the shade of a great oak tree that grew near the school. One day as he sat with a book open on his knees a mighty stag came toward him, laid itself down by his side, and offered its spreading antlers as a book rest! After that it came every day, and used to follow Ciaran about like a dog. Often he lodged his books in its antlers and had it carry them for him. On one occasion something startled the stag, which ran off with Ciaran's precious books in its antlers. That night it rained heavily, and Ciaran was worried that the rare and valuable treasures would be ruined. But when the stag returned not a single page was damaged.

Another time Ciaran was befriended by a fox, which used to take messages written on a slate between the youth and his master, Finnian. Wherever he was, animals and birds came to him, sharing in the gentle wisdom and kindness that were so much a part of his life. Even the trees in whose shade he so often sat seemed to bend down over him, offering deeper shade in the heat of the summer days, murmuring their songs to him as he sat lost in contemplation of some wondrous piece of knowledge.

One year, as the season turned toward winter, the school and the area around it suffered a famine. There was a mill attached to the school, and the pupils took it in turns to grind the grain to make bread. It was said that whenever it was Ciaran's turn, the Shining Ones would come and turn the wheel for him; but on this occasion, as Ciaran carried a heavy sack of oats to the mill, he exclaimed aloud, "How I wish this were beautiful wheat, so that I could make fine bread for my fellows."

When he reached the mill and opened the sack, it was filled with oats, which Ciaran poured into the quern. But as he turned the mighty wheel and milled the grain, it turned into the finest wheat. Filled with excitement, Ciaran carried home his sack of wondrous flour, and when he reached the school he went at once to the kitchen and baked some bread. Everyone who ate of it said it was the finest they had ever tasted, and when it was given out to some poor folk who came that way, it not only cured their hunger but made any who were infirm well again.

When Finnian heard of this he spoke the following poem of praise:

Ciaran, O great heart,
Grace will always be yours.
May you have an abundance
Of all good things.

Ciaran, blessed friend,
May all wisdom enrich you,
May your life ever be
Filled with wisdom and truth.

And soon after this Finnian, who was himself one of the wisest and holiest men in the whole of Ireland, had a vision. He saw two moons in the sky, one golden, the other of silver. Finnian declared that this referred to two great men who would be honored throughout Ireland and beyond and bring words of wisdom to many. "The golden moon is for one who shall be called Columbcille, and he shall make a foundation on Iona that shall live for a thousand years. The silver moon is for our own Ciaran, and he shall build a community at Clonmacnoise that shall be famed throughout the whole world."

When he heard this Ciaran was troubled, for he longed for nothing more than to live at Clonard and listen to the words of his teacher and to the songs of the trees. But in his heart he knew that the time was approaching when he must depart. Therefore he went to take his leave of Finnian, and promised him that whatever place he went, and whatever foundation he made, would ever be linked to his old master's school. And when he heard this Finnian wept with both joy and sorrow, and made a verse for Ciaran's leaving:

> A marvelous hero goes from us westward,
> Ciaran, son of the wright;
> Without greed, without pride, without anger,
> Without lust, without satire,

THE VISION OF THE GREAT TREE

So Ciaran set forth and for a time lived a wandering life. Everywhere he went miracles and wonders occurred, and he was remembered wherever he went with love and honor. One time he stayed for a time on the island of Aran, and there he helped dry the corn for the kilns belonging to one Lonnan the Left-handed. This man was ever somewhat jealous of Ciaran and liked to argue with him whenever he could.

One day as they were drying the corn they saw a ship foundering on the rocks near the shore. "Well," said Lonnan, "that ship will drown for sure—just as surely as this kiln will be fired by the strong winds that have brought death to the mariners."

"Not so," answered Ciaran. "The ship shall burn, but the kiln will be drowned."

"What nonsense you speak," cried Lonnan. But Ciaran's words were proved true, for even as Lonnan spoke a great wave lifted the ship and flung it down on the shore next to the kiln. Flames from the fire spread outward, borne on the wind, and within moments the ship was ablaze. But as for the kiln, and all the corn it contained, that was blown by the wind out into the sea and thus drowned, just as Ciaran had foretold.

After this Ciaran traveled to another part of Aran to stay with the wise and holy Enda. And there as they spoke of many things, including Ciaran's reluctance to settle and found a place where all could come and study with him, there came to both men at the same moment a great vision, which seemed to Ciaran as though it had been approaching him throughout his life.

In this vision they saw a great tree, mightier than any ever seen in Ireland. It grew on the bank of a stream, with its roots deep in the soil and its branches seeming to extend over more than half the land. It was laden heavily with fruit of the richest and sweetest kind, and birds and beasts and human beings came from all over the world to eat of them. When he saw this, Enda cried out for joy and said to Ciaran, "This tree signifies you and all the goodness and nourishment that you shall offer to the world. See, even animals and birds come to share the fruit of your tree! Observe well where it grows Ciaran, for on this spot you shall build a foundation that shall endure for a thousand years."

Ciaran heard the echo of Finnian's prophecy in these words, and shivered. In his heart he knew the truth of what Enda said. Moreover he knew the place where the great tree grew, at a place called Cluain, which lay almost in the center of Ireland. And so he departed from Enda with gentle words and set off to where he was to found his own place of wisdom and wonder.

CLONMACNOISE

So Ciaran traveled through Ireland and along the way he gathered about him seven companions, men who desired to learn from him and to help him in the work he was destined to do. For a time they lived on Inish Angin, and then at a place called Ard Tiprat, or "the Height of the Well." But at length they came to Clonmacnoise, and there Ciaran stayed.

Before he could begin building the foundation, he was required to ask permission of the local chieftain, Diarmit son of Cerball, a famous warrior. In this man Ciaran found an openness of spirit and a willingness to listen rare among fighting men. When Ciaran put his proposal to build a new foundation of learning and wisdom on his lands, Diarmit gave his permission at once. Then Ciaran looked at him and said, "Will you come with me and help me set up the first post in the enclosure?"

"Why do you ask me that?" said Diarmit.

"Because it is good that men of learning and kings should work together."

"Why do you call me a king?" asked Diarmit in surprise.

"Because by this hour tomorrow you will be king of all Ireland," answered Ciaran.

So Diarmit came with him and together they planted the first post of the enclosure. And that night the high king, Tuathal Marlgarb, was killed, and on the day following Diarmit was declared king in his place. Thus Ciaran's prophecy was proved and he earned a powerful friend in the course of it.

And so building went forward and within a year the foundation at Clonmacnoise was built. People began to come there from all over Ireland to sit at Ciaran's feet and listen to his wise words. And in token of the holiness of that place, and the vision he had received while on Aran, Ciaran planted a tree, which grew to a great height and offered shade to generations of those who dwelled in the foundation.

Ciaran declared that a fire should always be kept burning in token of the holy light that lived within the community. And thus it remained for several years, until it came into the mind of an evil man named Crichid to put out the flame. And this he did, and then ran away into the wilderness where he believed none would find him. There he met his death, caught and killed by wolves.

Meanwhile, at Clonmacnoise the loss of the eternal flame had been discovered. The brethren ran to Ciaran and told him what had occurred. He, rising to his feet, closed his eyes and cupped his hands as though to receive a gift. There, fire blossomed in his hands and amid cries of wonder, he carried it to the place where the flame was kept and lit it once again. Not so much as a scorch mark was on his hands, but the light that shone in his eyes was itself like a flame.

Not long after this, word came that Finnian had died in a plague then sweeping the country, and when he heard this Ciaran said, "I shall follow him soon." No one wished to believe this, for Ciaran was still a young man and strong. But less than a month after that he fell sick, and weakened rapidly. At this time he asked to be carried out into the open and laid upon the earth beneath the trees. Looking up at the sky through the dancing leaves, he said, "The way between the earth and the heavens is hard."

"Surely not for you, Ciaran," said his fellows.

"When I am dead," he said, "preserve the spirit of my teachings and not my relics. Let my bones rather be like those of a deer that lie all open to the sun and the rain. Let me lie beneath the tree I planted so that even in death I may share its joy and beauty."

Soon after this Ciaran breathed his last, and his body was taken to lie in the little church that he had helped to build. And but a day after that, Kevin of Glendalough came there, having heard in the songs of the birds he so much loved that Ciaran was dead. He went into the church alone and told all others to keep away. Then he sat by Ciaran's body and prayed for a while. And it is said that Ciaran's soul returned to his body for a brief time, so that he might speak with his great fellow.

The foundation of Clonmacnoise became one of the most famous in all Ireland, and ever the great tree watched over it, as the Shining Ones watched over all who came there in Ciaran's name.

❋ ❋ ❋

Despite the attention that the ecological movement has drawn to the plight of nature, we still take nature very much for granted. This was far from true in the world occupied by the Celtic saints. They, like their forebears the Druids and shaman-poets, were as close to nature as it is possible to be. They displayed a sympathy toward all living things, animals and plants alike, that was far deeper than a simple love of nature. For them the links were established at a soul level— hence the wonderful episodes that are to be found in virtually every history of the saints that has survived: stories such as those of Kevin of Glendalough's relationship to the blackbird, and of Ciaran's stag, which allowed him to use its antlers as a book rest, and of the vision of the great tree that impels Ciaran toward Clonmacnoise.

Ciaran's story illustrates the way that being in nature can teach as much or more than any formal learning, and that when the two things go hand in hand, the result is truly remarkable. Such a relationship with the natural world was an inheritance from earlier times, and is well attested in the fragmentary wisdom of the pre-Christian world, where a whole lore relating to sacred trees is to be found.

In Ireland, for example, there were five specifically named sacred trees: the Tree of Ross, the Tree of Mugna, the Tree of Dathi,

the Tree of Usnach, and the Tree of Tortu. The great compendium
of land lore, the Dinshencas, says of them:

> Eo Mugna, great was the fair tree,
> high its top above the rest:
> thirty cubits—it was no trifle—
> that was the measure of its girth.
> Three hundred cubits was the height of the blameless tree,
> its shadow sheltered a thousand:
> in secrecy it remained in the north and east
> till the time of Conn of the Hundred Fights.
>
> A hundred score of warriors—no empty tale—
> along with ten hundred and forty
> would that tree shelter—it was a fierce struggle—
> till it was overthrown by the poets.
>
> The Oak of Mugna, it was a hallowed treasure;
> nine hundred bushels was its bountiful yield:
> it fell in Dairbre southward,
> across Mag Ailbe of the cruel combats.
>
> The Bole of Ross, a comely yew
> with abundance of broad timber,
> the tree without hollow or flaw,
> the stately bole, how did it fall?

*These are enigmatic references, clearly allusions to cosmic
world-trees of the kind worshiped among the Norse as scions of
Yggdrasil, the World-Ash. Another text,* The Settling of the
Manor of Tara, *tells a wonderful story in which the chieftains of
Ireland, having come together to discuss the seemingly overlarge
dimensions of the Manor of Tara compared with their own lands,
desire to learn of the original reasons for the partitioning of the
land. To this end they summon two wise poets, who in turn
summon five older and wiser than they. None of these, however, is
able to answer, and all agree to summon the wise teacher Fintan,
who gives a poetic version of the history of Ireland.*

*He then goes on to tell the story of an earlier assembly of all the
kings and lords of Ireland, together with all their principal storytellers, brought together on the day of Christ's crucifixion by a wonderful being called Trefuilngid Treochair, "the Strong Upholder."*

> We beheld a great hero, fair and mighty, approaching us
> from the west at sunset. We wondered greatly at the magnitude
> of his form. As high as a wood was the top of his shoulders, the
> sky and the sun visible between his legs, by reason of his size
> and his comeliness. A shining crystal veil about him like unto
> raiment of precious linen. Sandals upon his feet, and it is not
> known of what material they were. Golden yellow hair upon
> him falling in curls to the middle of his thighs. Stone tablets in
> his left hand, a branch with three fruits in his right hand, and
> these are the three fruits which were on it, nuts and apples and
> acorns in May-time: and unripe was each fruit. . . . "I have

come indeed," he said, "from the setting of the sun, and I am
going unto the rising, and my name is Trefuilngid Treochair."
"Why has that name been given to thee?" said they. "Easy to
say," said he. "Because it is I who cause the rising of the sun
and its setting." "And what has brought thee to the setting, if it
is at the rising thou dost be?" "Easy to say," said he. "A man
who has been tortured—who has been crucified by the Jews
today—because of that the sun stepped past them after that
deed, and has not shone upon them, and that is what has
brought me here to find out what ailed the sun. . . ."

In the end Trefuilngid leaves Fintan some of the fruit from the branch
he carried, and it is from these that the five sacred trees grow.

Stories such as these emphasize the importance of tree lore and
the way in which it is intimately related to the mystery of life itself.
Trees are among the most ancient things on this earth, and as such
they represent ages of wisdom and knowledge. The Irish words for
"sacred grove" are fid-nemith or fid-neimid, which in turn derives
from an older Celtic word nemetos, meaning simply "holy" or
"sacred." This later became extended to mean a distinguished
person such as a poet, a king, or a wise dignitary. What image
could be more appropriate for Ciaran's ministry than that of a great
overarching tree? The links between these ancient living things and
the wisdom they have seen remain deeply rooted in our own time,
and can teach us, if we look closely at them, the eternal relationship
that exists between ourselves and the natural world.

▦ ▩ ▦

MEDITATION POINTS

- Consider your own relationship to the natural world. Go outside and really look around you. If you live in a city, find a park and walk there. Notice things about the trees and plants. Meditate on what you can learn from them. Remember that they are part of the cosmos as well as you.
- Ask what you can do for the natural world. Try to discover what it needs to restore the damage we have done to it.

▦ ▩ ▦

A Scribe in the Woods
A hedge of trees surrounds me,
A blackbird's song enchants me;
Above my lined page
Birds make a song for me.

The gray-mantled cuckoo
Sings in the bushes;
May God protect me—
I write well in the greenwood.

—*Ninth-century Irish; trans. J. M.*

CHAPTER 9

Son of the Star

Maedoc of Ferns

◼ ◼ ◼

Ath Ferna:
The place where Maedoc will dwell
Though filled now with litters of wolves,
Will offer songs to heaven yet.

—Betha Maedoc Ferna

*Maedoc, who was also know as Mogue and Aedh, was born in
Connacht at the end of the sixth century* A.D. *and died about 626. He
began his education in Leinster but soon transferred to the school
founded by Saint David in Pembrokeshire. After a number of years
there he returned to Ireland and founded communities at Drumlane
in County Cavan, Rossinver in County Leitrim, and Ferns in County
Wexford. Ferns has continued to be the place most closely associated
with him to this day. His staff, bell, and reliquary all survive and are
to be found in the National Museum of Ireland in Dublin and at
Armagh Cathedral. He is often remembered for protracted feats of
austerity, such as living on bread and water for seven years; but the
single most interesting aspect of his life is his visionary capacity, best*

displayed in the episode in which he climbs a golden ladder to speak to the departing spirit of Columbcille. In addition, his soul-friendships with a number of his fellow saints, including David of Wales, Molaise of Devenish, Columbcille himself, Ita of Killeedy, and Brighid of Kildare, show him to have been an important figure in the network of holy men and women who maintained the spark of the new faith within the Celtic countries.

As with so many of the Celtic saints included in this collection, Maedoc had a powerful link with the animal kingdom, being especially fond of wolves, and his protection of the hunted stag is yet another instance of the compassion toward other living things that set the Celtic saints apart from the rest of the people of the time, who hunted both for food and for sport.

The miraculous nature of Maedoc's birth, together with the title he received, "Son of the Star," shows him to have inherited, as did both Ciaran and Kentigern, something of an older tradition. The wonderful prophetic poem about Maedoc, attributed to the spirit of the great hero Fionn mac Cumhail, makes this clear enough, while the name suggests that he should be seen as a type of solar "Child of Wonder" and as a shaman-saint, able to move between levels of being and awareness just as the tribal shamans of many lands have always done and continue to do. Indeed, we can see a striking parallel between Maedoc's ascent of the ladder and the Siberian shamans' practice of shinning up the pole of a skin tent to look around them at the hidden realms, before returning with messages for the tribe. Like them, and in common with many of his fellows, Maedoc maintained throughout his life a deep sense of connectedness with the rest of the universe through accessing the invisible realm of the spirits.

※ ※ ※

SON OF THE STAR

There was once a king of Connacht named Setna, and his wife was Eithne. For years they longed for a child, but without success. Then one night both dreamed the same dream: that a star fell out of the heavens into Eithne's mouth. Each told the other of this, and together they went to the chief Druid to ask its meaning. The Druid looked into the place within and told them what he saw. "A child shall be born to you that shall be as marvelous a being as any that ever lived in Ireland." That same night a child was conceived in Eithne's womb, and in the fullness of time she gave birth to a son. On the night of his birth a ray of brilliant light rested upon the house where the woman lay in child-bed. It is told that on that same night, one of the Shining Ones known as angels came to Eithne and told her that her son should be a great worker of wonders. And it is also said that this being of light alone baptized the newborn infant, giving it the name Aedh.

As was the custom in those times, the child was put out to be fostered. The woman who cared for him, who was of the Ua Dunthaig clan, nurtured him as if he were her own and lavished love upon him. Her name for him was "My Little Aedh," which in the Irish tongue is written *mo Aed oc*. This name ever after clung to the child, and in adulthood he was known as Maedoc, so that his given name was all but forgotten.

FIONN'S PROPHECY

Meanwhile the Druid whom Setna and Eithne had consulted regarding the sign of the star had a dream of the child in which no lesser being than the great Fionn mac Cumhail, the greatest and wisest of warriors in all of Ireland, who had been dead for an age, came to him and put his thumb under his tooth of wisdom, by which means he used to discover all the knowledge of the world, and he said: "How glad I am that the place where my bones lie will be the center of learning and knowledge in Ireland. Many wise words shall be spoken in this place, and one who was but lately born shall speak of the mysteries of life there." And being a justly famous poet, Fionn made a song concerning all that he had prophesied, which the Druid set down when he awoke:

Ath Ferna:
The place where Maedoc will dwell;
Though filled now with litters of wolves
Will offer songs to heaven yet.

Ath Ferna of the green strand!
Excellent he who builds there;

Soul-friends will come there,
It will be a place dear to all.

Maedoc and his company shall come,
Like a glitter of sun after rain;
The Son of the Star will come,
Victorious over all adversity.

It will be a sacred place,
Where many great deeds shall happen;
Maedoc and his company shall come,
To welcome the mighty King of all.

He will be a strong and bounteous prince,
A flame of fierce consuming wisdom;
Maedoc and his company shall come,
Like a wave upon the land.

Thus the Druid wrote, and thus many years after he showed the writing to Maedoc himself, who had indeed come to Ath Ferna, which was known then as Ferns, just as Fionn prophesied. And when he heard this Maedoc smiled to know that the bones of the great hero lay beneath his foundation, and hoped that he felt joy in the words and songs that were sung there.

THE SONG OF THE STAG

But all this happened when Maedoc was in his middle years. Before then he had a journey to undertake, which took him far from his home and through many adventures laden with the wonder and wisdom of the inner life.

While he was still living in the home of his foster family he used often to spend time with the shepherds. One day, eight young wolves approached and fawned around Maedoc as though they were dogs. All were thin and wasted and when he saw them the boy's heart went out to them. "Take eight sheep from the flock," he said, "but see that you take no more than that." The wolves did as Maedoc had told them, and when the shepherds saw this they ran to tell his foster mother. She came forth in great anger and Maedoc fell upon his knees and asked that he be forgiven. When the woman came and counted the sheep there were the exact same number as before, and of the eight that had been carried off by the wolves there was no sign.

Soon after this Maedoc was sitting in a quiet spot in the woods reading when a stag came bursting out of the trees and fell down at his feet. Maedoc heard the sound of hounds in the woods coming closer so he placed his cloak over the horns of the stag. When the hunters arrived they saw only Maedoc and went on their way in search of their prey. When they had gone the stag arose and belled forth its wondrous song for Maedoc.

Another time a youth named Daimin son of Cairbre was drowned in Loch Erne but his body could not be found. His mother traveled throughout the land, visiting all the *Celli Dé* and asking them if they could tell her how to recover her son's remains. Finally Molaise of Devenish said to her, "The one called Maedoc shall come here soon, and he will help you."

So Daimin's mother waited there and one day soon the young Maedoc came that way. The woman fell at his feet and begged him to help her. Maedoc was still untried in his powers at that time, but her plea moved him so deeply that he begged the waters of the lake to give up the body it had claimed. And thus there came about a great wonder, for the waters of the lake parted and the body of Daimin rose up, and when he reached the shore he awoke as from a long sleep and was as whole as ever he had been.

At once the restored youth turned to Maedoc and greeted him as though they had been old friends, for even then the wondrous man used to walk in the realm of the spirits, and many who lived there knew him well.

The Transformation of Aed

After this, word of Maedoc's miraculous abilities spread far and wide and people began to seek him out to drink of his wisdom. But Maedoc became fearful of this attention and sought to escape to another place. It is said that he traveled to Rome itself and that in the Holy City the bells rang of their own volition when he entered there. Whether this is true or not I cannot say, but it is certain that Maedoc wandered the world for a time, and that in due course he returned to Ireland and settled for a time in Rossinver in the county of Leitrim. There it was that a certain king named Aed the Black came to him.

Now this Aed was hideous beyond measure, having suffered disfigurement in childhood. To Maedoc he said, "I have heard of the miracles you have wrought and I would ask you to do for me the greatest service possible."

"What do you ask of me?" said Maedoc.

"Give me a new face," answered Aed simply.

When he heard this Maedoc was troubled, for he believed that such an act as this could alter the shape of fate. But there was about Aed's wish a childlike faith, and he knew also that Aed was a powerful leader who might benefit the work he desired to do in Ireland. Therefore Maedoc called upon the help of the Shining Ones who watched over all that he did, and bade Aed lie down on the earth. Then he covered the king's head with the cowl of his own robe and sat by him through the night. When dawn came Aed arose, and he had upon him the face and form of a most beautiful man. Then he knelt before Maedoc and begged to be baptized, which the holy man did very willingly. Thereafter Aed took the name Aedan Finn (Aedan the Fair) to signify the new life that had come upon him, and he made over much of his wealth to Maedoc to begin building his first foundation of learning and wisdom at a place called Drumlane. Thereafter the two men became friends and ever after the king gave all his support to the work of the *Celli Dé*.

Maedoc in Wales

After a time Maedoc desired to leave Ireland and visit those of his brethren who lived in Britain. At first Aedan was reluctant to see his friend depart and did everything to prevent it, asking him to teach in various places and informing him of the needs for his miraculous work. But in the end Maedoc left quietly and found his way to the coast and so took ship for Britain. Once there he went into Wales and sought the school founded by David of Menevia. He was warmly welcomed and spent many weeks in contemplation with that stern and holy man.

The prior of David's church at that time was an envious man, and when he saw how much time Maedoc spent with his master he set out to damage their relationship by showing Maedoc to be lazy and shiftless. One day the brethren went out to the coast to collect firewood. But by chance Maedoc remained behind, reading in the garden of the monastery. There the prior found him and berated him for letting others do the work for him. When Maedoc showed his distress at this, the prior was glad. He bade Maedoc to make his own way to the shore and gave him a lad with an ox cart in which to carry back the firewood, secretly yoking two wild and unbroken oxen to the cart. When Maedoc came there the wild creatures became tame at once, and so they set forth. Soon they came to the edge of a bog that stood between them and the sea. The lad began to complain about the distance they would have to go to pass around the bog. When he heard this

Maedoc stretched forth his hand and a firm road opened before them. In wonder the lad drove the cart across the center of the bog and thus they arrived at the shore.

Meanwhile David came in search of his friend and found that in his haste to catch up with the rest of the brethren Maedoc had left his precious book open on the ground. At that moment it began to rain and David noticed that around the place where the book lay the ground remained miraculously dry. When he saw this he left the book where it was and set out to follow Maedoc to the sea. When he arrived he asked Maedoc sternly why he had left his book out in the weather, and the Irishman was so overwhelmed with grief that he fell down on the sand and would not get up again. After a time David and the rest of the brethren set out for home. On the way they learned from the lad about the new road through the bog land and at that David turned to speak to Maedoc only to realize that he was not there. No one had seen him since the incident on the beach, so all the brethren turned about and returned to where they had last seen Maedoc. There they found him, still lying upon the sand as if in a trance, while all around him great waves rose up and struck the shore, none coming near him at all. David spoke to him gently and related that his book was unharmed; then they all set off together for the monastery.

This was not the end of the jealous prior's evil deeds. So bitterly disposed was he toward Maedoc that he devised a means to have him killed and bribed a man to do the deed.

One day Maedoc set off alone to the woods and the man followed him. There he attempted to strike Maedoc down with an ax, but his hands stuck to the handle and he could nowise free himself until he fell at Maedoc's feet and confessed everything.

When Maedoc returned to the monastery alone the prior became fearful for his own life, and soon after he fled from the place. After he had gone the truth came out and David was mindful to set the justices upon him. Maedoc shook his head. "Do not trouble yourself, Master, the man will die a terrible death alone in the wilderness and none shall know where his body lies." And it is said that this came about just as Maedoc had foretold.

Thus he remained in Britain for a time, and did many wondrous deeds there, including healing the son of a king of that land who was both blind and deaf. But in time Maedoc longed to return to Ireland, and so he took leave of David and set out for home.

Maedoc of the Wolves

When he returned home Maedoc wandered for a time throughout Ireland, meeting and talking with others of the *Celli Dé*, especially Columbcille, with whom he became soulfriends. But in time he came to a place called Disert nDaibre, that is, "the Hermitage of the Oak Wood," and there he elected to remain for a time and build a foundation of learned men and women. One day, not long after the building had commenced, there came a pack of wolves to Maedoc's door and they each showed by sign and gesture that they were starving. Maedoc, mindful of that other time when he had given the gift of life to some wolves, granted them a single calf that belonged to the brethren. When his companions heard this they were dismayed. "The cows will not give milk without the calf," said one. Maedoc called this man to come close and placed a blessing on his head. "Now," said Maedoc, "go and milk the cows." And when the man went into the barn the cows all gathered about him and licked his head as if he were himself the calf, and they gave milk readily.

Not long after this Maedoc was on the road to visit a foundation at Shanbo in Leinster when there came to him a female wolf so thin that it could scarcely walk. Maedoc asked a boy who was accompanying him if he had any food to spare. The boy replied that he had a fish and some bread, but that they were for his master. Nevertheless Maedoc took them from him and gave them to the wolf, which ran off at once. The boy was now distressed at the trouble that would come to him, but Maedoc told him to bring some leaves from the forest, and when the boy did so he blessed them and they became a loaf of bread and a fish, which he gave with thanks to the boy.

A Time of Vision

Not long after this Maedoc was in a part of the land where the king of Ui Cennselaig was raiding. On a particular night this king fell sick and in his fever dreamed an evil dream: that he was taken to the mouth of a cavern, where fire and darkness awaited him. And there came forth a terrible monster that seemed as though it would eat him. Then there appeared a man who stood before the monster and commanded it to retreat so that the king was saved. When he awoke he was sore afraid of what this might mean and at the suggestion of his advisers he sent word to Maedoc begging him to come and explain the meaning of the dream. Maedoc came willingly, and as soon as the king saw him he cried out in wonder. For in Maedoc he recognized the same man who had saved him from the monster. At this same moment the king's sickness vanished, and in gratitude he promised to give Maedoc land on which to build.

The place chosen was Ath Ferna, or as it is more simply known, Ferns, and here Maedoc began to create the mighty foundation that he had always wished to have. One day the builders came to Maedoc and complained that there was not enough water to keep them all from thirst. So Maedoc told them to cut down a certain tree, saying that beneath it they would find a spring of pure water. This they did and the water proved to be the purest anyone had ever tasted, and it may still be seen today.

After this, building went ahead without interruption, and thus was Fionn mac Cumhail's prophecy that one called Maedoc would build there proved true, and in time Ferns became one of the greatest of such places in the whole of Ireland. As for Maedoc himself, this was a time of fulfillment and vision—fulfillment because he was at last realizing his greatest wish, and vision in that he had many such inner seeings in the years that followed. Of these, two will be remembered as long as people live in Ireland.

The first concerned the lineage of his old friend King Aedan, who had continued to offer support to all that Maedoc did. One day, through a gift of the Shining Ones, Maedoc saw a vision of all the members of Aedan's family, from the beginning of his line to the end, who would rule in Ireland for generations to come. Maedoc wrote them all down in a verse that is still known to this day. Part of it says:

Supreme rule for a time to them,
Three of them ruling over Ireland,

Thrice three over the province of Connaught.
Thrice five kings of them afterwards,
Will succeed—I remember their names:
Three Fergals, three Aeds,
Three Nials, many Ualgargs,
Tigernan, Amlaib, two Arts

Five Conchobars, two Cathals
and more. . . .

The kings who will succeed them,
Till the end of the world,
The name of each one will I relate . . .

In every case it came about as Maedoc foretold, and in
after years because of this he became known as a keeper of
ancestral wisdom. But the second great vision that is told of
him concerns not so much his own seeing as that of another
who saw him do a most wondrous thing.

It happened that Maedoc had gone to a high place to commune with the Shining Ones and the spirits of the great ones
of Ireland. Though he knew it not, a child followed him and
lay hidden in some bushes watching. And so it came about
that this child saw a golden ladder descend from the heavens
and watched as Maedoc climbed it until he could no longer be
seen. Long hours the child lay and watched and wondered,
until at last Maedoc returned by the way he had gone, climbing down the golden ladder, which then vanished from sight.
The child could keep silent no longer but burst forth from his
hiding place to demand where Maedoc had been.

"I will tell you if you promise never to speak of what you
have seen while I live," said Maedoc. And when the child gave
his word, Maedoc told him how he had been told that the
spirit of the great Columbcille had departed from life, and

because he wished very much to take leave of this wise and holy man, he had been granted permission by the Shining Ones to visit and speak with his spirit. As he had promised, the child never spoke of this until after Maedoc's death, when he was himself in the fullness of his years and gave an account of it, to the wonder of all who heard.

Not long after, Maedoc heard that he was to die within the year and that he should prepare himself accordingly. He did so, visiting all the communities he had founded and entrusting their continuance to those who shared his vision. To each he left relics: a bell to one, a staff to another, a book to a third. And then finally he returned to Rossinver and there died. But even after death his wonders continued. A man who had lain sick for almost thirty years had a dream in which he saw a chariot containing a man and a woman. When he asked who they were the man revealed that he was Maedoc and that the woman was no less than Brighid, and that they had come to bless him. The man recovered sufficiently to speak of this and then died peacefully. So for long years after, Maedoc was remembered and his vision kept alive among the *Celli Dé* and those who sought to drink of their wisdom.

※ ※ ※

Maedoc's life is one of deep vision, and it overlaps, to an unusual degree, with that of an older, pre-Christian society. His visionary abilities are such that one is reminded, again and again, of the old Celtic shamans, who like him had an understanding of the world of the spirits that enabled them to better experience the world about them. Maedoc's relationship with the land is profound. It enables him to make a fair pathway through a shifting bog and (in an incident not included in this retelling) walk on water. When he seeks to raise the body of the drowned youth, the waters of the lake give up their burden gladly. This act alone not only emulates the abilities of other great teachers to bring the dead back, but recalls the way in which the older shamans could identify the dead from a single bone. Daimin seems to recognize Maedoc, having, we assume, encountered him in his wanderings in the realm of the spirits. This knowledge seems to aid Maedoc in recovering the lost youth.

Indeed, if there is one single theme in the golden skein that is Maedoc's life, it is his connection with the ancestors. His birth is foretold by the great Irish hero Fionn mac Cumhail, in a poem that bears all the hallmarks of being genuinely old (perhaps adapted from another, older character to fit that of Maedoc). And, of course, he makes a great and extraordinary prophecy (extending to many more verses in the original) in which he gives an account of the entire lineage of Aedan, whose appearance he so dramatically changes.

This episode seems more reminiscent of pre-Christian magic than the work of a saint, and recalls a character known as Avagdu, or Utter Darkness, in Welsh mythology. This youth was so ugly that no one would have anything to do with him, until his mother, skilled in magic herself, sought not to transform his face but to give him wisdom instead, so that those who spurned his appearance would at least gain from his knowledge. It might be said that Maedoc acted unwisely in altering the king's appearance, which *after all followed a natural course of events; but he shows his deeper wisdom in looking beyond this to the good that will come of it. Aedan not only (according to Maedoc's own prophecy) sires a long line of kings, but also continues to support Maedoc in his work of creating monastic foundations, through which he is enabled to share his wisdom more widely.*

Of all the episodes in Maedoc's remarkable life it must be the one in which he is observed climbing a golden ladder to commune with the spirit of the recently dead Columbcille that marks him out as above the ordinary, and as a true inheritor of the Celtic shamanic tradition. As already noted, the practice of climbing the pole of a tent, or a mighty tree, was a symbolic act that the tribal shamans of old Europe undertook to give a visual aspect to their inner, spiritual journey. In fact, as they climbed they went into a light trance, which enabled them to travel out of the body and enter the realm of the spirit, where they received information relevant to the tribe whose spiritual welfare they oversaw. What, if anything, Maedoc learned from Columbcille is not recorded, but we may be sure that from the conversation of two such wise and holy men only something of a powerfully mystical nature could emerge.

In many ways, perhaps, Maedoc's life seems more remote than that of some of his brethren; but in fact we are all far more deeply connected to the realm of the ancestors than we realize. Modern shamanic practitioners, who have begun to apply the techniques of soul-work and healing to contemporary ailments, would recognize the importance of Maedoc's connections with the "great dead," as a means not only of maintaining links with the cultural history of the

Celts, but also of accessing knowledge and wisdom from the past
that might otherwise be lost.

Travel between the physical realm and that of the spirit was a
commonly understood and widely practiced event at the time in
which the Celtic saints lived (roughly between the second and the
ninth centuries A.D.). It was considered by no means strange or
unlikely for a person to apply to the ancestors, living or dead, for
advice—and in many parts of the world to this day it is normal to
pray to the spirit of one's grandparents or great-grandparents for
help in time of trouble.

For us today as individuals, no matter where we live, ancestral
links can reconnect us with the heritage of our own family and the
native culture from which we originate. Many contemporary forms
of illness have been traced back to events in the chain of family life
that have not been fully or even partly recognized. Such
fundamental problems as child abuse, incest, and the breakdown of
the family can be seen as originating in the ancestral past, and only
by accessing and exploring such unhealed wounds can we deal with
them effectively. Even the simple act of admitting a slight or injury
toward some family member, either now or in the past, can have an
immensely healing effect. At a deeper level it may be necessary to
forgive wounds dealt by ancestors who are no longer living—an act
that can have a profound effect on the individual at a soul level.
Unresolved conflicts can fester as deeply as any physical wound,
and the acknowledgment of such—often hidden—agendas, now or
in the past, releases us to continue living our own lives. By
considering our own relationship to parents, life partners, and

children—even those members of the family who are no longer alive—we find that things that have interrupted the flow of our own soul's journey can be healed and removed.

That Maedoc's experience reflects this shows up again and again in the story given here. His connection with the deep inner places of the soul, where matters of ancestral import are so often found to be the key, is what makes his story so important to our own continuing journey.

❁ ❁ ❁

Meditation Points

- What is your own relationship to your family?
- How aware are you of your cultural and ancestral roots?
- Are there unresolved differences in your family's past? How can you deal with these? Do they affect your own life today?
- Are there people to whom you should say you are sorry, either now or in the past?
- Are there ancestors of whom you are aware who have had a profound effect on your life?

❁ ❁ ❁

Recollections

God help my thought
That strays from me always;

I fear danger from it
On the day of judgment.

Through all the ways it goes,
Often down the wrong road;
Shouting, rushing,
Quarreling even before God.

Through thrusting throngs,
Through troops of women,
Through woods and cities,
Faster than the wind!

Now by straight paths,
Now by rough;
Harsh ways, easy ways,
I do not lie!

Wandering, it crosses seas
Without a ship;
Leaping in a single bound
From earth to heaven.

Unwisely running
Close and far,
After every excursion
It returns home.

I've tried to bind it
To fetter its feet;
But it's still not constant
Nor mindful to rest.

Sword and lash,
cannot restrain it;
As slippery as an eel
It eludes my grasp.

Neither lock nor prison,
Chain nor earth,
Fortress or sea
Will hold it fast.

Dear Christ, to whom
All is clear,
May a sevenfold grace
Keep and control it.

Govern my heart
Stern God of the Elements;
May we be together
In your enduring fire.

—*Tenth-century Irish; J. M., after Kuno Meyer*

CHAPTER 10

The Hospitality
of the Heart

Berach of Rathonn

❋ ❋ ❋

Berach the sweet-lipped
Left disbelieving brothers
Hospitality of a true lord. . . .

—Betha Berach

*We know less about Berach than about any of the other saints
gathered together in this book. The text of his life, the* Betha Berach,
*was, according to the colophon of the text, "copied from a bad old
vellum book, belonging to the children of Brian O'Mulconry the
younger . . . on Feb 6, 1629 by the poor friar Michael O'Cleary." On
the evidence of the text itself, Berach was born at Gort na Luachra
(the Close of the Rushes) near Cluain Conmaicne in Connaught. He
seems to have been roughly contemporary with Kevin of Glendalough,
although some years younger, since the foundation at Glendalough is
already functioning by the time he arrives. This puts him as alive in
the sixth century. Beyond this, we have no information other than
that contained in the text of his life, which remains one of the most
quietly powerful accounts of the Celli Dé that I have found.*

Berach's miraculous encounters with warriors mark one of the key themes in his story, as does his long quarrel with the poet Dairmait, which has a ring of historical truth about it. Berach is able, through the power of his faith, to transcend the petty squabbles of other men, and his actions at the battle of Cluain Coirpthe mark him out as a figure with powers every bit as effective as those of the Druids who were performing similar feats only a few years earlier. Among the many half-forgotten tales of the Celtic saints, Berach's deserves to be better known; it is hoped that its inclusion here will bring it out into the light of day again after many years of obscurity.

▩ ▩ ▩

In the Field of the Sun

When Patrick was bishop over all Ireland he went into Connaught and visited the house of Dobtha the son of Aengus. They gave Patrick a great welcome and Dobtha's wife told Dobtha to go and catch some game for the table. Dobtha and his sons went out at once and had better luck than ever before. When they returned it was almost dark, and though the entire household searched high and low they could not find so much as a single lamp or candle to light the house. Then it is said that Patrick worked a great miracle, for he called back the sun so that it shone briefly again over the land of Ireland. For this reason the spot where this took place is called Achad Greine, "the Field of the Sun."

Now the cauldron was set above the fire and Dobtha and his wife and sons and Patrick and his clerks gathered about it. And Patrick spoke the words of blessing upon the house and talked of the Great Mystery, so that Dobtha was moved to ask for baptism. But Patrick shook his head. "I will not baptize you, for a child shall be born to you and your wife, and of its line shall come another who will bring that gift to you himself. And I promise you further," he said, "that you shall not die until that child is grown and shall come to you with the blessing of God." Then the great saint made a further prophecy, which was that when the child of whom he spoke returned to that place he would build a great foundation on a nearby stretch of boggy ground. "That is a hard place to build," said Dobtha. And Patrick, with a flash of his eyes, answered, "What is hard for man is easy for God." Then he promised a gift to the child, that he should have the hospitality of the heart from all good men, and that each one should contribute a burning brand from their fires to his fire, and that he himself would contribute a brand from his own fire. Neither Dobtha nor his wife understood this promise at that time, but in days to come they would remember it and see how great was the foresight of Patrick.

THE BRIGHT YEARS

And so Dobtha lived on in the Field of the Sun, and his wife bore him three sons, one of whom, Nemhall, took a wife named Finmaith, who bore him a son that they called Fintan.

Many signs and wonders surrounded his birth, and before long all knew that he must be the wondrous child of which Patrick had foretold. So he was given into the care of a man named Fraech to foster, and he, in turn, gave the child a new name, Berach, which means "acute or sharp," for the clarity and sharpness of his wits were so great that all came to honor him for his wisdom even before he became a man.

When he was only seven years of age, Berach went to study with the great Daigh son of Cairell, who was noted for his wisdom and the depths of his teaching. And there, one time, came some distinguished guests. But all the household was away save for Daigh and Berach, so the youth washed the feet of the guests and then went to prepare supper for them. He found only a small sack of wheat in the storehouse, and even this needed to be ground before it could be used. Berach hurried at once to a nearby mill and begged the woman he found there to grind his wheat before the oats that she was about to grind. Not only did the woman refuse, but she spoke harshly to Berach and slightingly of his master. At this, Berach emptied his bag of wheat into the mill, and to the amazement and fear of the woman the mill wheel ground out wheat meal from one side and oat meal from the other, without mixing them at all!

At that moment the woman's husband and sons arrived and hearing what had happened threatened to kill Berach. But when he looked at them their weapons stuck to their hands and they could not move at all until they had begged his forgiveness and promised him no harm. Then Berach took his sack of milled wheat and went home.

BERACH AND KEVIN

When Daigh heard of these events, he said that Berach should no longer remain in his house but go at once to Glendalough, where Kevin would be his new teacher. Then he gave him a gift, a small bell that had great powers, having belonged to another holy teacher in the past. So Berach set out across Magh Muirthemne and by way of the river Boyne into Bregha. Along the way he passed through the lands of the king of Tara, who was preparing a feast for another king. Berach asked for a drink and was refused. "Well," he said to the steward who had turned him away, "the feast would not have been the less for the sake of one drink." Then he went on his way. But that night when the feast began it was discovered that the fifty vats of beer that had been set aside for the occasion were all bone-dry— though they had been full earlier. "Who has been near them?" demanded the king. The steward remembered Berach as the only other person apart from himself who had been near the vats. "Go after him," said the king. "But do not harm him. Ask him to return here and eat with us, and be sure to ask him politely."

The steward went after Berach and soon overtook him. Red-faced, he begged the youth to return and Berach did so. When he entered the hall he drew forth the little bell that Daigh had given him and rang it once. Its sweet chimes filled the hall and at once the vats were filled with the finest beer ever drunk in that place. Then the king asked for Berach's blessing and received it, and afterward he sent many provisions to feed both Berach and his growing company of followers in time to come.

Then Berach went on his way and soon arrived at Glendalough, where Kevin welcomed him warmly. But Berach saw that his host was troubled, and when he asked the reason learned that Kevin's cook had but lately died. Now he had guests and no one to prepare food for them. "Let me do it," said Berach.

In the kitchen he found scant food and drink, but what there was he gathered together on a great table. Then he divided the amounts exactly into two halves, one at each end of the table. Then he blessed each amount, and they became twice as much as before. Three times again he divided the food, and each time there was double the amount when he had blessed it. Then he prepared as fine a meal as had ever been eaten at Glendalough. When Kevin learned what had happened—knowing full well that there was little provender in the kitchen—he gave thanks to Berach and begged him to remain there as long as he wished.

FAELAN THE FOSTERLING

Now Kevin had a beloved fosterling, Faelan the son of Colman, who was himself son to the king of Leinster. A frail child, he was often heard crying for things he needed. One day he was crying out for milk, and at that time Kevin had none to offer him. When Berach heard this he raised a hand and blessed the mountain before him. Then he said, "Let the doe that is upon this mountain come hither." And the doe came and gave its milk for Faelan.

On another occasion Faelan was crying out for the healing plant called sorrel. This was hard for Kevin since it was winter and no sorrel grew at that time. But when Berach heard this he put his hand upon a certain rock, and at once sorrel sprang up through it and covered it. Many say that this rock is still there, and that sorrel grows upon it out of season every year because of the miracle of Berach.

Yet again when Berach himself was with Faelan the child cried out for apples. Berach looked around and saw only a willow tree growing nearby. "God can do even that," he said, and put his hand upon the trunk of the tree. At once a heavy crop of apples was upon the willow, and Berach plucked some and gave them to Faelan.

All these things were done because Faelan was a child of special promise who would one day himself be a leader and teacher of men. But he had a stepmother named Cainech, who had married the king of Leinster after his first wife, Faelan's mother, died. Now she had sons of her own, and when she heard of the wonders wrought for her stepson by Berach, she became fearful that he would displace her own children. Therefore she gathered about her a number of women of power and came to Glendalough with the intention of harming the boy. One of the Shining Ones came to Kevin and told him of this, and Kevin in turn told it to Berach to see what he would do.

At once Berach set out to meet the women. He came upon them at the top of a mountain and there addressed them, asking them to return home and to leave Faelan in peace. At this Cainech raised her hands to lay a curse on Berach, but he merely raised a hand against her and her companions and said, "Be under the earth." At once the earth opened and took them within the body of the mountain, after which they were seen no more.

The Battle of Cluain Coirpthe

For a few years more Berach remained at Glendalough, until Kevin said that he should go forth and make his own way in the world. "For it is time that you fulfilled the prophecy of the blessed Patrick," said Kevin. Then he had all Berach's things placed in a chariot and summoned a stag to pull it. "Wherever this stag shall stop there shall I remain and build my foundation," said Berach. Then he set forth with his attendant, Maelmothlach, and some others who wished to go with him from Glendalough. Many days they traveled, until at last the stag came to the edge of a wide plain, and there it stopped and lay down. "This is the place where we shall stay," said Berach, and he sent Maelmothlach to explore the area.

Very soon the attendant returned with grim tidings. It seemed that a battle had been fought in the fields that very day and a great slaughter made. "This is a terrible place," said Maelmothlach, "a place of death and corruption." Berach opened his eyes very wide and looked away into the distance. "It shall be called 'the Meadow of Corruption,'" he said, "lest anyone forget it." Then he went forth onto the field and found there a fort over which the battle had been fought. And when he had stood and contemplated it for a time, and walked among the dead and dying who lay upon the field, Berach began to work a wonder of the greatest kind. Circling the field he chanted aloud and blessed all who were there. And where he walked men rose up that had been dead and stood blinking in the sunlight. And at the center of the field he came upon the bodies of the two princes who had fought there. They were Donnchad of Tara and Tipraite son of Tadg from Cruachan. These two also Berach healed and to Tipraite he gave back life. And he made peace between them.

Afterward a poet among the hosts made a song of the battle, which said:

Donnchad and Tipraite,
Both their great forces
Fell in the wide enclosure,
At the center of the fort;
Every mantle was torn
Every shirt bloody

Every wound inflicted.
Until there came
Berach of the fair face
And woke the sleepers
From the place of death.

After the two princes made peace, they went their ways, leaving Berach to begin the work of clearing the land and building upon it. And soon, when the work was completed, came Berach's old foster father, Fraech, and his teacher, Daigh, and they blessed and consecrated the foundation. Also it was at this time that Berach journeyed to the place where his grandfather Dobtha, now greatly aged, was still living. There, just as Patrick had foretold, the old man received the sacrament of baptism from the hand of his grandson, and soon after he died peacefully and was laid to rest in the graveyard of the monastery.

THE POET'S CHALLENGE

But Berach's tenure in that land was not to be easy, for there lived at that time in the same place a poet named Dairmait, who was mighty in both song and druidcraft. He had made a song praising Aedh, the king of Connacht, and the king had rewarded him with a gift of land that included the place upon which Berach had begun to build. When he heard this Dairmait grew angry and sent word to Berach to leave. Berach refused, saying that Patrick himself had chosen this spot for him and had prophesied that he would occupy it.

The two men met under a certain thorn tree at Rathonn, which was sacred to Dairmait, to discuss the matter. But they could not agree, and so they went before King Aedh and asked for a judgment. But secretly Dairmait told the king that if he chose in favor of Berach he would satirize him in such a way as to raise boils on his face. The king knew that this was no idle threat, for such was the power of poets in those times. He also feared Berach for the miracles he had performed. Therefore he refused to give judgment in the matter.

Berach and Dairmait searched the length and breadth of Ireland for someone who would give a judgment for them, but they found no one who would do so. "Let us go to Alba, to the land of the Scots," said Dairmait, "for there we shall certainly find one wise enough to settle this heavy matter."

Berach agreed. They went first to the fort of Aedan mac Gabran, one of the high chieftains of Scotland in that time. It happened that a great feast was about to begin, so that many young warriors were out in the meadows below the walls of the fort trying their hand at various sports. Dairmait hurried ahead of Berach and spoke to them. "An impostor is coming," he said. "Attack him with cudgels and dung and stones." And, because Dairmait was finely dressed and Berach only in a simple robe, the warriors believed the poet and hurried to attack Berach. When he saw them coming he held up a hand and said, "May you be unable to do what you intend." At once all the young men stopped still as if frozen and could not move a muscle.

Dairmait glowered at this and hastened on. Soon the two men stood before the gates of the fort and Dairmait pointed to two mounds of snow that stood on either side of the entrance. "If you were any kind of a holy man you would make fire of that snow so that we could warm ourselves."

"Let fire be made of them," said Berach. "Go and blow on them, O poet." And Dairmait went and blew upon the snow and it burst into flame. Then he was silent.

Meanwhile, these deeds had been noted by the servants of King Aedan, who asked his Druids what manner of man this visitor was. The Druids went into the inner place where visions are found and returned with knowledge, which they gave to the king in verse:

> There is no noble shining saint
> Who could attain such deeds
> Save Berach the triumphant
> From fair Rathonn.
>
> Berach, son of Nemhall
> Son of Nemargen of heroic strength
> Is no landless man,
> His power is mighty
> When he puts it forth.

His swiftness is revealed,
He turns away evil,
Bright gold his breast
As the morning sun.

When he heard this the king ordered that Berach and Dairmait be admitted to him, and he honored them both. To Berach he offered land in Scotland to found another monastery, and this Berach promised to do, leaving behind some of his followers to begin the work. Then both he and Dairmait laid their grievance before the king, who after a time gave as his opinion that only one man was wise enough to make a judgment in the matter of the land, and that was Aedh the son of Brennain, the king of Tethba.

So Berach and Dairmait the poet returned to Ireland and went to Tethba and asked the king for a judgment. And the king declared that an assembly should take place at Lis Ard Abla, that is, "the High Fort of the Apple Tree," to discuss the matter. But when they came there, and many other of the *Celli Dé* and the high lords of Ireland also to hear the judgment, Dairmait began to revile Berach because they were not meeting beneath the thorn tree at Rathonn, which being a sacred spot to him he thought the only place where they might speak together without anger. And Berach looked at Dairmait and said, "Then let the thorn tree be brought hither." And in a moment, to the wonder and terror of all who were present, and most especially to Dairmait, the tree was carried through the air and settled in the earth beside them.

When he saw this the king declared that he could make no judgment, since a higher authority than his had already made itself known. This only made Dairmait angrier than before, and he rose to make a satire upon Aedh. Then Berach stepped forward and placed a hand over the poet's mouth. "Neither satire nor praise-song shall pass your lips until the day you die. And that I declare shall be within a year."

At this Dairmait could no longer hold out against the power of Berach, and he bowed his head and departed. When he was gone the thorn tree once again lifted itself into the air and went back to Rathonn, where it is said that it may still be seen to this day. And Berach gave thanks to the king of Tethba and at that moment, the young warriors, who had remained unmoving all this while in far off Scotland, were released. Berach then returned home. Soon after, Dairmait left the land for which he had fought, though he continued to live nearby and whenever he could lost no chance to revile the name of Berach. But in all that time he was unable to compose a poem, either a satire or a praise-song.

And so the days passed until it was almost a year since the day of the assembly, and Dairmait was heard to say with a sneer that Berach's prophecy was not going to come true.

But later that day, as the evening was drawing in, there came a great commotion outside Dairmait's house, and he went to look out. There he saw a group of hunters, who had cornered a stag just below his window. Even as he stood there one of the huntsmen flung a spear, which missed the stag but struck Dairmait instead, killing him outright.

Thus was Berach's prophecy proved true, but the matter did not end there. For Dairmait had a son named Cuallaid, and when he heard of the manner of his father's death he rose up in the spirit of vengeance to curse Berach and the land over which the poet and the wise man had fought. He set out with nine others to curse Rathonn, so that no corn would grow there, and the cows refuse to give milk, and the trees in the woods remain leafless.

When Berach heard of this he sent a trusted attendant, who was named Concenn, to challenge Cuallaid and his followers before they could do any damage. "See that you offer them no harm," ordered Berach. But Concenn did not do as his master had bidden. He was a wild-tempered youth, and when he saw the poet's son coming along the road in his chariot he hid in some bushes, and when the chariot drew near he threw a spear, which struck Cuallaid on the head and felled him to the earth.

Concenn fled when he saw the result of his actions, while Cuallaid, who felt his death approaching, ordered his men to carry him to a certain hill from which he might overlook Rathonn and curse it still. But when he came to the top of the hill he was too weak to stand, and with his failing sight could see only a single clump of oak trees. These he cursed with his last breath, and ever after they would bear no fruit or leaves, but stood as though dead.

Then Cuallaid's men went to Berach and begged his forgiveness, and he was much saddened by Concenn's actions, and spoke of his regret for all that had happened through the quarrel over the land.

With the matter thus ended, Berach worked hard to bring his vision into being. Many people came from all parts of the land to hear him speak, and many brought brands of light and understanding from the fires of their hearts, so that the words of Patrick long ago, that Berach should have a flame from the fires of many men, were finally understood. And ever were Berach's words of forgiveness, and of the hospitality of the heart that all men should have toward one another.

Berach lived to a great age and performed many more miracles that are recorded in the books of the *Celli Dé*. But one remains that must be told here since it speaks so well of the great wisdom possessed by Berach.

Once there was a famine in Ireland, and many went short of even a crust to feed themselves. In the lands next to Rathonn lived a man named Laegachan, whose wife was heavy with child. One day Laegachan went out in search of food, and he said to the woman before he departed that if she bore the child while he was away she should kill it, for they had nothing with which to feed it. And not long after he was gone the woman bore the child indeed, and it was a boy. The woman could not bear to kill it but devised a plan to save its life by taking it to

Berach, for she knew that he would not refuse to care for it. So she gave the babe to one of her women, who went to Rathonn and told Berach what had occurred. When he heard this he wept openly. Then he said, "Take the child back to its mother. Assure her that the means to feed it shall be found."

So the woman returned home with the child, and as she entered the house there came a great noise outside. Everyone rushed forth to see what had caused this, but they could see nothing. This happened twice more, and on the third time they saw an otter dragging a mighty salmon, the largest anyone there could remember seeing, toward the house. When it saw the people it ran off, and they pulled the huge fish inside and cooked and ate it. And there was sufficient meat on the fish to last them several months, by which time the famine had passed. Later, when the child was grown to manhood, he came to Berach and served him faithfully until the time of his death.

On the day long appointed, one of the Shining Ones came to Berach and told him that his time was come to pass out of the mortal world. And it is said that Berach went willingly and with a smile on his lips, leaving behind a great foundation where the wisdom he had taught was remembered and shared with all who came there for many generations afterward.

❈ ❈ ❈

The story of Berach is only a small step away from the great mythic stories of Ireland. Although he is a wise and holy man, Berach's powers extend far beyond those normally attributed to the Celli Dé.

In the episode of the battle of Cluain Coirpthe, for example, he is able to raise the dead to life again and thus to end the conflict that might otherwise have brought a shadow upon the land where he intended to build. Later we read of Cuallaid's curse, which is recognized as real enough to blast a clump of oaks, though the land about them is spared. Such curses are common in the heroic literature of the age, but it is rare to come across one in the life of a saint.

Berach's long-standing feud with the poet Dairmait has a ring of authenticity about it. According to the complex laws of the time, Dairmait probably had every right to be where he wanted to be, but the earlier prophecy of Patrick is seen to take precedence over the gift made by the king. Their long search for a judgment shows how delicate the balance was between pagan and Christian communities in the Celtic world, and illustrates as well the power possessed by the poets at that time. In order of precedence, poets ranked only third in importance to the king himself, and such were their powers that it was widely believed that a satire could actually have physical results, such as the raising of boils on the face. This was called a glam-dichenn, *and one of the most celebrated is described in an ancient text known as* Cormac's Glossary. *Here the satirist is the famous bard Nede, who makes a satire against King Caier that is recorded as being:*

> *Evil, death, and a short life to Caier;*
> *May spears of battle slay Caier;*
> *The rejected of the land and the earth is Caier;*
> *Beneath the mound of the rocks be Caier.*

Next morning when the unfortunate king went to wash he found that three discolorations had appeared on his face—one crimson, one green, and one white—signifying disgrace, blemish, and defect. Since the law of the time stated that no king bearing a disfigurement of any kind could rule, Caier was forced to flee and Nede became king in his place.

While the struggle between Berach and Dairmait never goes this far, it is a serious matter for all that, and Berach's final prohibition, that no poem or songs should come from the mouth of his enemy, is a terrible one indeed.

The two central themes of Berach's life revolve around justice and blessing. We see him overcome opposition by recourse to the law, as in the case of Dairmait, or as in the instance of the opposing warriors at the battle of Cluain Coirpthe, he brings justice to them by working through what we might call "natural" law. This same theme comes out again in the whole matter of the judgment before King Aedh, who in the end refuses to cast his vote either way since a power greater than his has already decided. In our own lives we see this happen again and again, in cases where we think we have the right, or see that another is in the wrong, only to have circumstances change the direction of our thinking.

The blessings that Berach offers are manifold, and range from the miracles he performs for the child Faelan to the way that he is able to defend himself from unworthy attacks by simply blessing the space before him or the people in question. Thus he brings the doe from the mountain to feed Faelan and stills the warriors of King Aedan by the simple raising of a hand.

Indeed, most of his miracles draw upon the natural world in one form or another, and like so many of the Celli Dé he has an important relationship to the animal kingdom, as is evident in his calling the otter to bring the huge salmon for the starving family.

But perhaps the most wonderful image in the story is the prophecy of Patrick and its eventual fulfillment. Patrick promises that Berach's fire will be fed with brands from many fires, and this is indeed so. His own light is a single flame, but from the flames that grow independently around him a greater fire is created. We can learn from this the importance of combining and sharing our individual flames, which together make something more than we could ever produce on our own. Others can take fire from our example as we live our lives to the best of our abilities. Berach offered the hospitality of the heart to all who came to him. In our own lives the magic of the heart-fire will be perceived by others as a warmth and inner strength that draw them to us naturally as friends and co-workers. If you know someone in your life who is like this, a gentle being around whom others constellate, then he or she is more than a little like Berach.

⬛ ⬛ ⬛

Meditation Points

- What is the spark of divine fire in you, and how does it manifest?
- How strong is your sense of justice?

- Consider an event in your life in which you feel you were unjustly treated and ask yourself how this came about. See past your personal point of view to the point of view of others.
- Look about you and try to find someone who naturally draws others to him or her by the light of an inner fire.
- Is there poetry in your life? If not, how can you manifest it there?

❈ ❈ ❈

God of the Moon

God of the moon, God of the sun,
God of the world, God of the stars,
God of the waters, the land, and the skies,
Who ordained for us the King of Promise.

It was Mary fair who went upon her knee,
It was the King of Life who went upon her lap,
Darkness and tears were set behind,
And the star of guidance rose early.
Illumined the land, illumined the world,

Illumined both doldrum and current,
Grief was laid and joy raised up
Music was played on bright harp-strings.

—The Carmina Gadelica

CHAPTER 11

THE DEER'S CRY

PATRICK OF ARMAGH

✠ ✠ ✠

Come hither, Patrick, hither come!
Shield of the Gael, thou light of story
Appointed star of golden glory!

—*Anon.; trans. Robin Flower*

Patrick is something of an enigma. Despite his fame, the details of his life are so contradictory that it is hard to arrive at an accurate picture of him. He is famed as the first and greatest bishop of Ireland, yet he may well have been self-appointed and never actually have been consecrated in this office at all. (Indeed, there is some doubt whether he was even a monk.) He is famed as the patron saint of Ireland, but he was born in Britain of Welsh and Breton parents. He is the only one of the Celli Dé who left a partial account of his own life—the Confessions—*although it has been so often misquoted and edited that few would now recognize the original. Yet for all this, he remains a shining light among the stories of the Celtic saints, and his inclusion in any collection such as this one is inevitable.*

Even Patrick's dates are doubtful, although most authorities now place his birth at about A.D. *390 and his death at about 461.*

His father was a decurio (town councilor) and also a deacon in the local church. His mother, whose name may have been Concess, remains a dim figure in the background.

They lived in a town called Bannaven Taburniae, in the area of Strathclyde. Captured by pirates and taken to Ireland while still in his teens, Patrick returned to Britain and was trained in the rudiments of Latin theology (he later bemoaned the fact that he had not received a better education).

Returning to Ireland in about 435, he established a base at Armagh, which has continued to claim him as its patron ever since.

Doubt overhangs Patrick's death as it does much of his life. The fact that the exact place of his burial remains unknown has enabled several rival churches to lay claim to his relics. Glastonbury in Somerset, famous for its connections with the Arthurian and Grail legends, claims that he came there for a time—although in fact it was probably another Patrick who did so. Eight early churches and foundations in Britain and another three in Wales are named after him and claim connections with his life. He is the primary patron of Ireland, and in our own time his feast day, on March 17, has become something of a major holiday, especially in the United States and Australia, where families of Irish descent have made his day their own. The main cathedral in New York City, which is dedicated to Patrick, organizes the great parade that throngs that city's streets each March.

His legendary struggle with the pagans of Ireland may not be all it seems; as with much of his legend, it has been rewritten to suit the needs and wishes of later generations. It is far more likely that

Patrick felt a certain affinity with the Druids he is generally depicted as fighting. As is true of several of his fellows, Patrick's own powers are equal in every way to those of his adversaries and every bit as magical.

Patrick's life is, like those of his fellows, full of wonder and miracles. But there is another Patrick who lingers beneath the more colorful aspects of his legendary self. It is that of a sincere and essentially simple man, whose generosity of spirit so impressed his contemporaries that they treated him as a saint virtually within his own lifetime. The story he tells in his own words confirms him as both likable and honest, a seeker after truth whose example still shines out to all who are dedicated to the soul's continuing journey today.

❈ ❈ ❈

Fire and Water

Even before birth Patrick wrought a wonder. His father was Calpurnius, of the Strathclyde Britons, and his mother was Concess, daughter of Ochmass, who hailed originally from Lesser Britain. In the early days of her pregnancy Concess entertained a certain king, washing his feet and giving him wine to drink and bread to eat. The king was moved by her beauty and looked with longing upon her, so that his wife, the queen, became eaten by jealousy. Secretly, she prepared poison and gave it to Concess in a drink. But the child, waking in the womb, seized the dark draft and turned it into a stone. When Concess in time gave birth to a healthy son, he was born holding the stone in his hand.

Near to the place where he was born lived a wild youth named Gornias, who was blind. He had a great reputation as a seer and wise man, and Patrick's mother wished to take her son to be blessed by him. When they reached the cave where Gornias lived, he came forth to meet them, clad in skins. He turned his blind eyes toward the child and blessed it. Then he said, "This child will outreach all others in this land. His name shall be remembered throughout Ireland and beyond." Then he turned away and spoke no more, though it is said by some that he regained the sight of his eyes thereafter.

When it came time for Patrick to be fostered, as was the custom in those days, he went to live with his mother's sister, who was barren. One day, as winter loosed its grip upon the land, a great flood came into the house where they lived. The hearth fire was quenched and all the vessels and gear of the house were afloat in the water. Seeing this, Patrick cried out that he was hungry and began to weep. His foster mother reproached him, saying, "How shall we make food without a fire? We have troubles enough without this!"

Then Patrick stopped crying and a light came into his eyes. He gathered some dry straw and, standing on a dry place, dipped a hand into the water. Five drops ran from his finger ends and as they fell they became sparks of fire. The straw caught and blazed up and Patrick fed the flames with tinder and flakes of wood. The water came no higher, and while the child laughed in delight his foster mother watched in wonder.

Nor was this the only time that Patrick showed himself master of fire. Another time his foster mother asked him to fetch faggots for the hearth fire. Patrick went forth and returned with handfuls of icicles gathered from the doorsill. The woman scolded him, saying, "These will not warm us!" But Patrick answered, "If we only believe it, these icicles will flame like withered wood." And as he said this he threw the ice into the fire and it blazed up at once.

Not long after this, it happened that some children in the village where Patrick dwelled brought fresh honey to their mothers—all save Patrick, who returned empty-handed. "Why do you not bring me honey?" said his foster mother. Without a word Patrick rose and took a vessel and went outside to the well. Filling the jar with water he blessed it and brought it back inside, where it was found to be filled with the finest honey imaginable.

After this, his foster mother sought to test him. It happened that a woman who used to work alongside her in the milking sheds had a child that died. As the woman mourned, Patrick's foster mother told her to bring the dead infant to the milking place and to lay it in the straw alongside the cattle. Then the two women began to milk the cows. In a while Patrick came there and his foster mother gave him a foaming jug of milk to drink. "Call that other boy to share the milk," she said, and watched to see what Patrick would do. Without hesitation he called to the dead boy. "Come, share my drink." The dead child awoke and rose up and came to him and was fulfilled. The women were filled with wonder and knew that the prophecy made by Gornias had already begun to be true.

Capture and Restitution

When Patrick was little more than thirteen years of age he traveled to Lesser Britain with his parents to visit his mother's family. It so happened that four sons of the king of Britain had been exiled to that land, and out of anger and frustration they ravaged the towns and villages in the area. In the fighting that followed, both Calpurnius and Concess were killed, and Patrick together with his sisters Lupait and Tigris were captured and taken by ship to Ireland, where they were sold into slavery to different masters.

Now there followed a period of seven years, during which time Patrick grew to manhood and served his master so well that he received nothing but praise. Miliuc was his master's name, and he was king over Dalraida and a harsh but not unjust man. Yet, though Patrick suffered no more than the loss of freedom, ever did his heart yearn for his homeland, and he continued to mourn the deaths of his parents and the loss of his sisters.

Patrick's chief task was caring for his master's large herd of sheep, and this placed him often alone in the wilder part of the lands over which Miliuc ruled, especially near the woods of Fochlad. There it was that he began to discover a part of himself of which he had hitherto been only half-aware. The wonders he had performed as a child had passed him by; he scarcely remembered them as more than dreams. Now he began to sense the world around him to be full of a wonderful energy of which he himself was a part. Day after day, as he sat watching over the sheep, he began to walk deeper and deeper into the secret places of his soul, and there it was that he encountered a presence that, though it had neither face nor name, he came to recognize as other, separate from himself. Soon it spoke to him, teaching him the ways of wonder, enriching his life and deepening his awareness of the living world.

At length a time came when Patrick could no longer remain silent with all the thoughts that were within him, and he began to speak of what he had learned, at first only to his fellow thralls, then to the children of his master, who having heard him speak, returned to listen to his words.

So the time passed until it was the seventh year of his captivity, at which time, as was the custom, a bondsman might be set free. Miliuc, who grew daily more conscious of the value of his slave, took thought as to how he might keep him longer. To this end he purchased a bondswoman, whom he gave in marriage to Patrick on condition that he remain in service for a further seven years. When he saw the woman Patrick noticed a white scar on her brow. "How came you by that mark?" he asked.

"It was when I was but a child," the woman answered. "I fell and struck my head upon a rock. My brother, who possesses the skill of healing, laid his hand upon me and I was restored." Then Patrick wept, for this was indeed his own sister, Lupait, who had been carried off into slavery with him.

The next day as he watched over the sheep the inner voice spoke to him, saying: "The vessel is prepared for you. Drink and set forth, for the world has need of you."

"I shall not go without my master's leave," replied Patrick, and the voice was silent.

So Patrick went to Miliuc and asked his leave to depart.

"You may go, but you must pay me a gold piece for your freedom," replied his master.

Then Patrick returned to the wild lands and spoke with the inner voice, telling it what he must do to earn his freedom.

"Tomorrow, when you return this way, a boar will come," said the voice. "Watch how it digs in the earth. It will turn up the treasure you require."

Patrick did as he was bidden, and sure enough when the boar dug in the earth it turned up gold enough to purchase not only his own freedom but that of his sister. And so the two left that place and set out for Britain. There Patrick was joyously received, and as the people became acquainted with his wisdom they begged him to stay there and to teach. But Patrick found that his heart was restless, and the inner voice spoke to him of far-off lands and the learning that he might find there. And so he took ship to Gaul and there found his way to the foundation of the great Germanus, who instructed him in many wondrous things and encouraged the gift that was within him to grow and flourish. But ever it seemed to Patrick that he heard the voices of the children he used to teach in the woods of Fochlad calling out to him: "We beg you, holy boy, to walk among us again!"

Return and Resistance

So it was that Patrick set out again to return to Ireland. But this time he came in triumph, and of his own free will. And when he was close to the mainland he saw a little island rise from the sea close to his ship. On it were two people, a man and a woman, who seemed aged beyond the years of mortals.

"Who are you?" cried Patrick.

"We have been here time out of mind," said they. "We await the coming of one who will set us free."

"I am that one," said Patrick, for his inner voice told him this was so.

Then the ancient ones wept and gave to him a staff carved with intricate designs. "This shall be your sign," they said. "Take it with our blessing." And Patrick took the staff and went on toward the land.

He landed at the place that nowadays is called Inispatrick, whence he went to stay in the house of a worthy man named Sescnech. This man had a young son who, when he saw Patrick, was so enchanted by him that he would not leave his side. That night he would not sleep with his father or mother, but chose instead to lie on a pallet next to Patrick. In the morning he clung to the visitor and would not be parted from him. When he saw this, Patrick blessed the child and bade him wait until he might come and be with him for as long as he wished. "For this shall be the first of my followers," he said, and indeed in time to come the child, whose name was Benen, became his foremost attendant, and remained with Patrick until the day of his death.

Once word got out that a new and wise teacher had come into the land, people came from all over to hear him, and soon Patrick had a large following. Then he set out to visit the king of that part of Ireland, a fierce warrior named Loeguire son of Niall, to ask permission to teach and build in his lands.

It so happened that Patrick came to Tara of Bregh, where the king held court, on the eve of Loeguire's feast day, at which time he had given forth a decree that no other fire might be lit in all the land until he had lit the fire of celebration in Tara. Patrick, ignorant of this edict, kindled a blaze on the Hill of Fiacc, and there celebrated the mysteries of Christ.

When word of this came to Loeguire, and he saw for himself the pinpoint of fire on the distant hill, he was greatly angered. "Who dares to defy me in my own land?" he demanded. And one of his Druids, overhearing this, quoted to him a prophecy that had been made three years earlier:

The Adzeheads will come over a furious sea,
Their mantles over their heads,
Their staves crook-headed,
Their tables in the east of their houses.
All who hear them will answer: Amen.

"This is one of those who were prophesied," said the Druid. "They will destroy you and all your kingdom if they are permitted to remain. Also unless this fire is put out tonight it will continue to burn for a thousand years."

Then Loeguire was troubled indeed, and summoned his war-band and his chief Druid, Lucetmael, and they set forth at once to confront Patrick. He, when he saw a forest of torches and a glittering of spearheads coming toward him across the plain of Tara, went to meet them.

"Who are you that dares to light a fire in my land on this night?" demanded Loeguire.

"I am called Patrick. I seek to teach and build schools in this land."

"You shall not do so while I am king," declared Loeguire. Then suddenly he gave a signal and his war-band advanced.

When Patrick saw this he called upon the power that lay within him and raised the staff he had been given by the undying folk of the island. At once a cloud of absolute darkness descended upon the king's men, and the earth shook beneath their feet so violently that they began to flee, stumbling and falling upon one another in the impenetrable gloom.

Then Loeguire cried out, "Let us talk!" and at once the shaking ceased and the darkness retreated. Then the king called for wine and bade Patrick sit down with him. But as the cup was passed from one to another the Druid Lucetmael spat into it. When the cup came to Patrick he blessed it and the liquid at once turned to ice. Then he upended the cup, and a single drop of spittle fell out, the very same that Lucetmael had put in. Patrick blessed the cup once more and the wine became liquid again.

Then Lucetmael rubbed his hands and said, "Let us work wonders on this great plain."

"What kind of wonders?" demanded Patrick.

"Let us bring snow over all the land," said the Druid.

"I shall not do anything that is contrary to the law of God," answered Patrick.

The Druid then began to work his magic, and in a while snow lay over all the plain, a foot deep, so that all marveled.

Patrick looked at the snow and said, "Very well. Now take it away again."

"That I may not do," said the Druid, "until morning."

"It seems you can only manage half a task," said Patrick, and as he spoke the snow began to melt away, until the plain was clear again.

Then the Druid summoned a darkness of his own, but Patrick dispelled that.

Things might have continued in this way for much longer, but at last the king himself declared that both should undertake a test to see who was the stronger. The test was to be an ordeal of fire and both agreed to attempt it. Loeguire called upon his men to build two huts, one made of green wood, and the other of dry wood. Then he declared that Patrick should go into the dry hut and the Druid into the green hut. This they did, and the huts were set on fire. The green hut in which the Druid sat was consumed, and he with it; but the hut made of tinder-dry wood in which Patrick sat would not even catch fire at all.

When he saw this the king acknowledged that Patrick was a man set apart, a veritable Druid, and swore that he would trouble him no more, but that he might be allowed to teach and go wherever he liked. Secretly, however, he planned to lay a trap, and to kill Patrick and all who followed him.

Next morning Patrick and his followers set out to cross the plain of Tara. As they came to a place where rocks lay tumbled about the earth, the inner voice that went always with him spoke to Patrick and warned him that Loeguire and his men lay in wait for them. Then Patrick summoned up all his strength and made a great invocation, which may still be heard on the lips of men and women to this day. Thus he spoke:

I gird myself today
With the strength of God,
With God's might to uphold me,
God's wisdom to guide me,
God's eye to look before me,

God's ear to hear for me,
God's words to speak for me,
God's hand to guard me,
God's way to lie before me,
God's shield to protect me,
God's host to save me,
From all who might harm me,
Both near and far,
One or many. . . .

As he spoke these words Patrick and his companions took upon them the appearance of deer, and so passed through the ambush without harm. From which cause to this day the invocation of protection is know as "The Deer's Cry."

DEATH OF A LEGEND

After this King Loeguire troubled Patrick no more but allowed him to go where he would and to do what he wished unchecked. And so the word of this great new teacher began to spread throughout Ireland until there was scarcely any place where his name was not known and his deeds not celebrated. Wherever he went he taught the wisdom he had learned in the wilderness, and built foundations and schools where the word of God might be spread abroad.

In Armagh he built a great church, and ever afterward the people of that place claimed him for their own. But it was not intended that Patrick should die there, nor for his bones to lie where any man might discover them. For, when he was old beyond the years of most mortals, and felt his death come near, he set out for Armagh, being at that time in the county of Derry. But the voice that had spoken within his soul so often before reproved him, asking why he undertook this last journey without its guidance. It told him that he should remain where he was until the hour when his soul must leave his body. Then the voice said, "Let two wild oxen be set free to wander upon the road, and, wherever they stop, let that be the place of your burial."

"It seems," said Patrick with a sigh, "that I have ever been in thrall." But he gave instructions that all should be done as the voice had told him, just as he had always done, and when the moment of his death came, it is said that a great light shone around his body for two nights. Afterward, the oxen were released as Patrick had requested, and they stopped at a crossroads midway between the lands of Derry and Ulster. There Patrick was buried, though in later times it is said that his bones were taken from there to another place. It is wisely said that he, whose name shone like a star over all Ireland, should remain hidden in the land, so that no place may claim him for its own.

※ ※ ※

Patrick is a man under orders. Right from the start, when he is recognized by the strange blind youth Gornias, he is set apart, and later, when he becomes a slave, he begins to learn about the hidden depth of the spirit under the guidance of an inner voice. He emerges from the state of imprisonment—which is metaphorically of the soul as well as the body—with new insights and ever-deepening wisdom. He is not only a wise and powerful teacher, but a natural magician also, one of whom the term shaman *could very fairly be used. This may seem at odds with the more usual portrait of Patrick, yet every incident told in the foregoing story is recorded in one or another of the lives that tell of him.*

The truth or otherwise of these stories is not in dispute; that he was perceived in this way by those who followed him is an indication of the person he really was. Episodes like the one in which he conjures fire from water (five drops: a significant number to the ancient Celts), or receives the gift of his staff from the undying people on the island—an episode that might have come from any one of a hundred Otherworld adventures of more ancient heroes— point to his unusual nature.

Patrick has always been represented as a hero, a soldier of God who faces the unfriendly kings of Ireland with their wonder-working Druids and wins; who brings the dead back to life and calls the elements to serve him at will. The extraordinary way in which he escapes the trap set for him by changing himself and his companions into the shape of deer is both a measure of his mature power and an interesting reflection of a more ancient practice. The Deer's Cry recalls a druidic method of shape-shifting called the Fith-Fath (pronounced fee-faw*) in which the person who wished to become invisible recited a charm and took* *on the shape of a beast. Patrick, as in the earliest instances in his life, uses druidic magic for his own protection, invoking his God in the same way that his forebears invoked theirs. To this day people make prayers of this kind, which are often called a Lorica or Breastplate, to invoke protection against all kinds of dangers. The ancient poem that follows at the end of this chapter is a striking combination of pagan and Christian imagery, as powerful a plea to the universe as Patrick himself might well have uttered.*

The very striking ordeal by fire that he undertakes as part of his struggle with the Druid Lucetmael is also part of an older tradition, which is recorded in a text known as The Irish Ordeals. *In this a number of tests and trials are listed:*

Mochta's Adze. *It was put over a fire of blackthorn until red hot, then passed over the tongue of the person suspected of falsehood. If it burned, the person was guilty; if not, the suspect would be freed.*

Sencha's Lot-Casting. *Lots were cast out of a fire. If the accused was guilty, they clung to his palm; if not, they would fall to the earth. Sencha used to make a poet's incantation over them.*

The Vessel of Badurn. *Badurn was a king whose wife had entered a faery mound and obtained a magical crystal cauldron. If three untruths were uttered in its presence, it would burst asunder. Then, if three truths were uttered, it would reassemble itself.*

The Three Dark Stones. *Three stones, one white, one black, and one speckled, were put into a bucket filled with black stuff from a bog. If the accused was guilty, he would bring out the black stone; if innocent, the white; if only partially guilty, the speckled.*

The Cauldron of Truth. *This was a vessel of silver in which water was heated to boiling point. The accused then put in his or her hand and if scalded was deemed guilty; if not, innocent.*

Luchta's Iron. *This sacred iron, brought back from Brittany by Luchta the Druid, was heated and put into the hand of the accused. As in later, medieval tests, if the iron burned, the accused was deemed guilty; if not, innocent.*

Waiting at an Altar. *In this ordeal the accused had to go nine times around the altar before drinking a cup of water over which an incantation had been chanted. If the accused were guilty, their guilt became manifest upon them. We are not told how this happened, but presumably either the guilty fell dead or they were forced to speak the truth.*

What Patrick's ordeal is telling us is that he cannot be killed because he still has work to do—indeed, his work is only beginning at this point. From here on, he blazes a trail across Ireland with his inspired teachings—his response to the needs of the people who enslaved him, the Irish, whose voices he hears calling out to him to "walk among us again."

The invisible bond between Patrick and his former captors is teased out by divine inspiration, leading him to return to Ireland. We do not know if those who came to hear him knew of his own story and past status as a slave. If they did, they would have been impressed by his courage in coming back to serve the land where he had been held captive, for they loved above all to hear stories of heroism, especially those where failure, sorrow, and difficulty caused the hero to persist in impossible service.

   Patrick's complaint of always being in thrall is a complaint that arises in even the most committed individuals—there is never enough "personal time or space" for those who are dedicated to spiritual service as Patrick was. How we can find ways of reinventing our work, of refreshing it and re-inspiriting it with meaning, is something his story can show us. We need to take time out to be quiet and contemplative, without the stimulus of books, music, or TV—to come again into the forgotten country of the soul. We need to spend time "in the wilderness," learning the old truths that are still there within us but may have been forgotten in the rush to succeed, to endure the pressures of life. Patrick's growth into his own spiritual journey, from the carefree wonders of his childhood to the sustained and conscious acts of his later years, reminds us of the journey we must all follow, and from which we can learn every time we stop to consider it.

❊ ❊ ❊

Meditation Points

- When did you last make time for inner work in your life?
- Consider what you can do to improve your ration of personal time.

- What kinds of things inspire or motivate you to make greater efforts?
- Ask yourself if you are in service to anything outside your ordinary daily activities.
- Try creating your own Lorica or Breastplate, for use in moments of doubt and fear.

⌗ ⌗ ⌗

Lorica

I invoke the seven daughters of Ocean
Who weave the threads of the sons of age.
Three deaths be taken from me,
Three lifetimes be given me,
Seven waves of surety be granted me.
No illusions disturb my journey,
In brilliant breastplate without hurt.
My honor shall not be bound by oblivion.
Welcome age! death shall not corrupt the old.

I invoke the Silver One, undying and deathless,
May my life be enduring as white-bronze!
May my double be killed!
May my rights be upheld!
May my strength be increased!
May my grave not be dug!
May death not visit me!

May my journey be fulfilled!
I shall not be devoured by the headless adder,
Nor by the hard green tick,
Nor by the headless beetle.
I shall not be injured by a bevy of women
Nor a gang of armed men.
May the King of the Universe stretch time for me!

I invoke Senach of the seven aeons,
Fostered by faery women on nurturing breasts.
May my seven candles never be extinguished!
I am an indestructible fortress,
I am an unassailable rock,
I am a precious jewel,
I am the prosperity of the weak.
May I live a hundred times a hundred years,
Each century in turn,
The fullness of their brew my sufficiency!
The encircling of the Spirit's fortress be about me!

—*Anon., eighth century; trans. Caitlín Matthews*

CHAPTER 12

The Well
and the Salmon
Kentigern of Scotland

❈ ❈ ❈

Power of wind be thine
Power of sun be thine
Power of water be thine
Power of earth be thine.

—*Gaelic incantation*

Historically, little is known about Saint Kentigern, beyond the fact that he was probably born toward the end of the sixth century A.D., that he was a bishop, and that he spent most of his life bringing Christianity to the Celtic tribes in the area of Strathclyde. Yet traditions concerning his life abound, including two versions of his life and several fragments that together build into a rounded portrait of an extraordinary man whose ability to see into the heart of things gave him prophetic powers and the gift of healing. His story is often considered to be connected with the life of the famous poet and prophet Myrddin, better known to us as Merlin, the archetypal wizard of King Arthur's court. There may, indeed, be some truth in this, as Kentigern was almost certainly a

*contemporary of both Myrddin and the historical Arthur. Lailocen,
the wildman who may have been Merlin, suffers the same threefold
death as the great enchanter—a death generally given only to
Druids or people of power.*

*According to widely held tradition, Kentigern (whose name
means "Hound-Son of the King") was believed to be the illegitimate
son of Urien of Rheged, a semihistorical figure in his own right who
turns up again in the romantic stories of Arthur as a king and
warrior and is present also in the early history of Merlin. The same
sources relate that Kentigern studied with Servanus, a sixth-century
Scottish bishop whose own life is as vague as his pupil's but who
may have been the apostle to the Orkney Islands.*

*Having created a foundation in the Strathclyde area Kentigern
is said to have run into difficulties with the local leaders and to have
been exiled to Cumbria (or possibly North Wales) where he founded
a monastery said to have numbered nearly one thousand monks.
Later he returned to Scotland and lived at Hoddam in Dumfries and
at Glasgow, the city that has claimed him as its own and contains
his relics in its cathedral of Saint Mungo (an alternative name for
Kentigern). He is believed to have died in 612, possibly aged eighty-
five—although this too may be apocryphal. Many of the people and
places mentioned in the story are real—Rederech was a real king
who ruled over part of Strathclyde in the sixth century, and Kings
Morken and Caswallen are both known historical personages.*

*Whatever the truth about the life of this passionate and
extraordinary man, his life offers a picture of magical and wondrous
events, from which—especially in the episode of the healing of the*

wildman Lailocen, and the many elemental aspects of his life—we may draw patterns of healing and vision for our own lives.

⬚ ⬚ ⬚

HOUND-SON OF THE KING

In the dark days after the departure of the Legions, King Loth ruled over much of northern Britain. A proud, harsh-natured man, he had one daughter, Tanau, whom he prized above all things. This girl had a simple heart, and when she found herself to be with child, though no man had known her, she believed that one of the Shining Ones had come to her and given her the gift of a baby. But when the king learned of her state his anger knew no bounds, and when neither threats nor cajoling would persuade her to give up the name of the man responsible, Loth, raging, insisted that she be given over to the justices to suffer the harsh penalty meted out to unmarried women found to be with child—that she be taken to a high point and flung down to her death.

Tanau bore all the slights and torments of her captors with fortitude, believing herself chosen to bear a wondrous child; and only when she was taken to the summit of the hill called Traprain Law did she utter a prayer that if her own life was not to be spared, then at least that of her unborn child might be. Her pleas fell upon deaf ears, however, and she was placed in a chariot and her hands bound to its rails. Then, at a signal from the judges, the chariot was pushed off the top of the hill.

The chariot should have fallen and smashed both itself and the body of Tanau on the rocks below, but instead—wonder of wonders!—it touched the earth as lightly as a feather, and the bonds that held the king's daughter fell away as though they had never been. Tanau stepped away from the chariot without so much as a scratch upon her, while those who had gathered to watch her execution stood amazed.

When Loth heard what had happened his anger was even greater. He gave it as his belief that his daughter had escaped owing to some evil magic. And, though many people thought that he should have taken note of the wonder that had befallen and set Tanau free, instead he decreed that she be subjected to a further ordeal—to be placed in a coracle and set adrift in the open sea. "If she be worthy of life," he declared, "her God will save her."

Thus Tanau was taken to the mouth of the river named Aberlessic and placed in a small skin boat without oars or rudder. This in turn was set upon the outgoing tide, which soon carried it from the shore. And many there noticed a strange thing. The mouth of the river had long been known as a place where fish were to be found in great numbers; yet when the coracle bearing Tanau was carried out to sea, the fish followed it as though escorting the craft, and ever afterward it was said that the waters thereabouts remained unproductive of fish.

For three days and three nights the frail craft was carried on the backs of the waves, with Tanau huddled in the bottom. In all that time she never once cried aloud with fear or doubt, being sustained by an inner sense that all would be well for her and the child she carried. Thus the morning of the fourth day dawned, and the coracle was cast up on the shores of Cullenross. Weakened by lack of food and water, Tanau crawled ashore and fell into an exhausted sleep. There she was discovered by some shepards who, seeing that she was near to her time, carried her to their own shelter and cared for her until she gave birth to a boy of great beauty and sweetness.

Then, consulting among themselves, and having heard something of her story, they decided to take her to the wise teacher Servanus, who was at that time living nearby. When he saw Tanau with the child she bore in her arms and the light that shone from both mother and child, he took them in. "For," said the wise and holy man, "I believe there is a great future for this small one." The child he baptized forthwith, giving him the name Kentigern, which means "Hound-Son of the King," though whether he came by this name through vision or by other chance I cannot say.

CHILD OF WONDER

Tanau and her child were given into the keeping of certain holy women, and when the child reached an age at which he might be instructed in matters of the spirit and the world, Servanus himself took over Kentigern's education, finding in him a willing and able pupil who soon showed himself as remarkable as the wise teacher's perception had foreseen. Many stories are told of those early days that give witness to the youth's wondrous nature.

At that time there were some ten other youths who studied with Servanus. Kentigern was not popular with his fellow pupils, who perceived him as a favorite of their master. Thus they ever schemed to do him ill, and behind the back of their teacher bullied and tormented him in any way they could. In spite of this, Kentigern retained a sunny temperament and spoke no harsh words against his companions.

Now Servanus had a tame bird, a robin, that came to him every day and in many ways exhibited its love for him. On one occasion the students captured this bird and began to make sport of it. It happened, however, that the bird was injured, and in its terror fell dead. The pupils, fearful of the anger they knew that Servanus would visit on them, sought to blame Kentigern, who had in fact taken no part in their cruel sport. When he saw what had occurred he took the dead bird in his hands and sought to warm it with his breath, praying over it with closed eyes. To the wonder and fearfulness of Kentigern's schoolfellows, the bird's heart began to beat again, and it flew from his hands to see its beloved master.

After this the youths hated Kentigern even more, and gave thought to how they could bring him into disrepute. Now it was his task to see that the rush lamps be kept alight in the little church where Servanus gave blessing and teaching to the people in the area, and he invariably rose early in the morning to see that the wicks were trimmed and the oil replenished. One day the other pupils woke even earlier and crept into the church to douse all the lights. When Kentigern came later he found the building cold and dark, with no fire from which to take a light. Concerned, he wandered out into the predawn stillness and found himself by a stream on the banks of which grew a hazel bush. As he looked upon it a light was kindled in its heart, and filled with wonder he drew forth a single branch, which at once burst into flame between his hands. Joyfully Kentigern bore the light back to the church and lit all the lamps, at which point the branch ceased to burn. Afterward he planted the hazel bough close by and it is said that in time it grew into a stand of hazel trees that always had a light about them as though warmed by an inner glow.

THE WAY AHEAD

After this the other pupils hated Kentigern more than ever, and strove to make his tenure with Servanus daily less pleasant. Finally, after several more months of this, Kentigern looked within and found the vision to depart the place. Not wishing to bring hurt to his old tutor, he left secretly, at night, and followed a wandering path until he reached the banks of a swift-flowing river. There, as he hesitated over which path to take next, the waters were divided, and there before him stood one of the Shining Ones, beckoning him across.

Filled with wonder Kentigern crossed the river dry-shod, and thereafter the river flowed back and rose so high that it burst its banks and spread over the land on either side, making it impassable to all. But as Kentigern stood and watched all this, he saw the bowed figure of Servanus approaching the farther side.

"Would you go without even taking your leave?" Servanus called sadly.

"I sought only to give you less pain," answered Kentigern.

"Have you forgotten everything that has been between us?" said Servanus. "How you came to me as a child, and how you have learned from me ever since. Indeed, I am more father to you than any other living man."

"It grieves me to leave you," said Kentigern with tears in his eyes. "But the time has come for me to seek out my destined way. These waters that are between us are a token of this. Neither of us may cross them, and I must go my way and you yours. But do not think that I love you any the less because of this. I know now that I have always awaited this moment, and that the time has come for me to follow the path ordained for me."

Then Servanus wept openly. "It is as you say, and I know this also. Nevertheless my heart is heavy. Go with God, my son, for I see that the way is clear before you."

Servanus turned away and went back to the school where he had lived and taught for so long. Soon afterward he died, some said of a heart broken by the departure of his beloved son Kentigern.

KEПTİGERП THE BİSHOP

For a while now Kentigern pursued a wandering way. In time this brought his steps to the place called Glasgow, and to the door of a house, within which he found a man close to death. When the man saw Kentigern he called out his name, then told him that a vision had told him that a man bearing his name and face would come, and that only when he had received Kentigern's blessing could he die. Much moved by this the youth blessed the sick man, who died forthwith with a smile on his lips.

Kentigern saw this as a sign that he was destined to remain in Glasgow, and since the sick man had gifted him with all his worldly possessions, he had the wherewithal to begin creating his own place. In the next year he began to build a church and outbuildings to house those who would soon come to study with him. Stories of his miraculous powers and spirituality spread quickly through the northern lands.

It was said that when he celebrated the mysteries a light often shone out from him, and that on occasion a white dove flew down and settled on his shoulder. Wherever he went he read the mysteries of the elements, speaking of the beauty of air, fire, earth, and water. Another time when he needed to plow a field and had no cattle, he called upon two mighty stags and harnessed them to his plow. Later, one of the stags was attacked and killed by a wolf, and when Kentigern saw this he called upon the wolf to submit itself to him. This it did and, to the wonder of all, Kentigern harnessed the remaining stag and the wolf together, causing them to pull the plow in harmony.

It was this act alone that caused the people of Glasgow to ask Kentigern to be their bishop, and despite his protests that he was still too young, they would not accept his refusal. Soon after, at the age of twenty-five, he was duly consecrated, and began at once to pursue his ministry with sincerity and devotion, seeing to the building of churches and the foundation of several new monastic settlements.

So for a time all was well with Kentigern, and word of his wisdom spread throughout the land. But soon the old king died and a new leader, named Morken, took his place. This man was powerful and greedy, and had no love for the *Celli Dé*. Thus he took to speaking ill of Kentigern, calling him a sorcerer and an evil magician, and impugning his works. For a time Kentigern was able to ignore this, but matters came to a head when, seeking provender for his numerous and widespread followers, he approached the new king with a request for grain.

"I have none to spare," declared Morken, whose barns were in fact bursting. "And even if I had I would never give any to you."

But Kentigern persisted gently, explaining his needs in greater detail, until at length the king shouted at him to leave.

"If your wisdom is so great see if you can move the contents of my barns to your own place without my help. If you can perform such a miracle you may have anything you can get!"

Quietly Kentigern took his leave and returned to the settlement at a place named Mellindenor, on the river Clud. There he spent time in prayer and meditation. Soon after this the river began unexpectedly to rise. In the city where King Morken held sway it burst its banks and, islanding the royal grain store, lifted the barns from the earth and bore them away, depositing them finally at Mellindenor, where Kentigern gave thanks and dispensed the grain—miraculously dry despite its journey by water—to those who needed it.

After this King Morken felt only hatred toward the wise bishop, and on an occasion soon after when Kentigern visited the royal palace, Morken became so enraged that he kicked out with his foot and laid the bishop on the earth. Kentigern himself made no complaint, despite the anger of many of his followers. But soon after this Morken's foot began to swell with gout, and in less than a year he was dead.

Many saw this as a judgment upon him for his insult to the holy bishop, and though Kentigern himself offered prayers for the dead man's soul, Morken's family was filled with hatred for the bishop and sought for ways to destroy him. Twice attempts were made on his life and in the end, at the insistence of his followers, Kentigern departed from Glasgow and fled into Wales, where he was made welcome by the blessed

David. Here also the king, Caswallen by name, made it known that he rejoiced to have Kentigern in his realm, and offered him lands on which to found a new community.

Kentigern, joyful in this news, traveled to the lands offered to him. There, accompanied by a number of his most devoted followers, he wandered through the lands seeking a sign of where he should begin to build his new foundation. And there, as they walked near a grove of trees, came a great white boar that circled them for a time and then finally came and laid its head on the earth before Kentigern. He, touching its bright wicked tusks, followed where it led, to a sheltered place in a thickly wooded valley. "Here," he said, "we shall build." And he blessed the boar, which at once ran off into the trees and was seen no more.

So work began at a pace, with trees felled and foundations dug. Then came the local prince of that land, Galganau by name, who demanded to know by what right Kentigern should build there. Even the name of King Caswallen had no effect upon this proud man's heart, and he ordered his soldiers to burn down all that Kentigern and his followers had built. But as he rode away Galganau was struck by a sudden blindness, and in fear he was brought back to the bishop, who stroked his brow as he had stroked the white boar's tusks, at which the prince's sight was restored.

After this there was no further opposition to the work of Kentigern and his followers, and in a while the foundation began to grow and flourish, with people coming from far and near to stay there and to listen to the inspired teachings of Bishop Kentigern.

For a time the foundation had no name, but it acquired one in remarkable circumstances. Kentigern was given to meditation and prayer in the open air, sometimes sitting for hours together, unmoving and unconcerned by the weather. On one occasion the air was so bitterly cold that the holy man nearly froze. It was thus that one of his youngest followers, a boy named Asaph, found him. When the youth saw that his master could scarcely move for the cold, he ran back to the monastery and, hastening within, took two hot coals from the fire and ran back with them in either hand to where Kentigern sat. With the coals he made a fire and slowly Kentigern was freed from the spell of the cold. As for Asaph, his flesh was not at all burned by the carrying of the hot coals, and when Kentigern heard of this wonder he declared that the foundation was to be named after Asaph. Many years later the boy would himself become the leader of the community, and longer still after that it is known still as Saint Asaph's.

THE RING AND THE SALMON

After this Kentigern remained in Wales for a number of years, growing wiser and more beloved every day. At the end of that time he received word that a new king, Rederech, now held power in the northern lands, and that this king desired greatly that Kentigern return to his old place at Glasgow. And, since the foundation of Asaph was well established, Kentigern agreed, and having made Asaph himself the foundation's new leader, he set off for his native lands. There he received a tumultuous greeting from the people, and both the king and his queen, Languoreth, came forth to welcome Kentigern.

Not long after this there occurred an incident that is listed among the greatest of the wonders performed by Kentigern. The queen had fallen in love with a young soldier in her husband's guard, and in a moment of foolishness gave to him a ring that the king had given her. The soldier, proud of this love-gift, took to wearing the ring, and it was not long before another of the king's servants saw and recognized it. Immediately he went to Rederech and told him of this evidence of the queen's infidelity.

At first the king was reluctant to believe this talebearer, but when he saw the ring he became first suspicious and finally convinced. As soon as he could he organized a hunting trip and took the soldier along with him. There, as the young man slept under a tree, Rederech took the ring and threw it into a nearby river. Then, on his return, he asked the queen, in seeming innocence, where the ring was that he had given her.

Turning pale, Languoreth said that she would search for it, that she believed it put away in one of her jewel boxes, and at once sent a secret message to the soldier to return her ring.

When he confessed that it was missing the queen knew that she was doomed, and threw herself upon the king's mercy.

Rederech was unmoved, and demanded that his queen be taken into custody and tried for treason and adultery. It was only as she languished in her prison cell that Languoreth thought of Kentigern. She sent a message begging him to come, and in due course the now-aging bishop arrived. The queen confessed her guilt and begged him for help, promising never to give way to such foolishness again. And Kentigern, who saw that in her heart she still loved the king, and remembering perhaps his own mother's punishment for transgressing the laws of men, promised to do what he could.

Returning home he instructed a messenger to go to the nearby river and there to cast in a line and bring to him the first fish he caught. The man obeyed and soon returned with a large salmon. Kentigern took a knife and, opening up the fish, withdrew the very ring that the king had thrown into the water. This he sent secretly to the queen, who at once summoned her husband and showed him the ring. Without this evidence Rederech was forced to pardon his wife, and in truth he was well deposed to do so, for he too still loved the queen and had feared to see her punished.

Only long years after, when King Rederech was dead, did the queen tell of Kentigern's part in the affair, and it was counted among the many wonders that he performed in the twilight of his life.

THE BISHOP AND THE WILDMAN

One of the last of these wonders concerned a strange wild-man called Lailocen, which some believe to have been a name adopted by no lesser figure than the seer Merlin, whom madness had taken after he witnessed the terrible carnage at the battle of Arderrydd. It happened that Kentigern used to walk often in the quiet of the woods near his home, listening to the songs of the birds and the murmur of water from a spring that rose in the depths of the forest and was believed to possess healing properties. But one day when he approached this place he found that another was there before him—a strange figure clad in skins with long, matted hair and beard. He looked at Kentigern with wild, blank eyes and then ran shrieking into the trees.

After that he was often there when Kentigern came to the spring, and though at first he always ran off, in time the presence of the bishop no longer seemed to worry him. Indeed, when Kentigern made no attempt to communicate with him, the wildman gradually began to look for his coming, and finally learned to sit with him, absorbed in the tranquillity of the spot.

At last, one day he spoke, in an old cracked voice, rusty from lack of use.

"What are you?" he asked.

"A man, just like you," answered Kentigern.

Bu the wildman only shook his head at this, and ran off.

Next day, however, he returned, and Kentigern was able to speak with him again, gently encouraging him to reveal more of his nature. Eventually the wildman's story was pieced together: how he could no longer stand to be in the world of men after seeing his fellows slain in battle. Now he lived in the forest, his only companions the trees and the wild animals whose society he sought in preference to that of men.

As the two men spoke more, Kentigern learned that the wildman called himself Lailocen, and that he had a gift for prophecy that was perhaps part of his madness. Many things he told the bishop as they sat together listening to the voice of the water. Then, one day Kentigern asked the wildman if he wished to be healed, and to live among his own kind again.

"At times I grow weary of birdsong and beast-grunt," Lailocen said.

"Then drink from the wellspring, for I believe it can heal you."

Slowly Lailocen looked at the water welling forth, then at the face of his companion. Slowly he put his hands into the water and cupped them and brought water to his mouth. As he drank his eyes became clear again and he looked with wonder at his surroundings and at his own wild state.

Gently Kentigern took him by the hand and led him back to his own home. There the wildman remained for a time, as his spirit slowly returned to him. But though healed in body and mind, he retained the gift of prophecy—though it was ever after a wild and uncertain gift, which led him to speak often in words that few could understand. Indeed, his hold on reason was slender, and at times he would revert to his old wild ways—though he never again strayed far from Kentigern, who seemed much like a father to him.

Years after, when Kentigern was celebrating the mystery of the Eucharist, Lailocen sent word that he was shortly to die. He asked for a blessing from the holy bishop and sent also a strange message.

"I shall die today in three ways: for I shall be stoned, pierced, and drowned."

When he heard this Kentigern and all those with him shivered, for such triple deaths were not unknown in those days, and always presaged the passing of a great one.

Kentigern sent his blessing to his old friend, and heard later that he had indeed met his end as he had prophesied, for some servants of a man that Lailocen had offended by telling him of his wife's infidelity set upon him and stoned him. Struck repeatedly, the wildman fell over a steep bank of the river, where a sharp branch pierced his body. As he fell back dying, his head went beneath the water and he drowned. Thus was Lailocen's last prophecy fulfilled, and in token of the friendship that had been between them Kentigern saw to it that he was laid to rest beneath the trees of the forest, close by the spring where they had so often talked.

Not long after this Kentigern himself, now of great age and venerability, died. His last words to those who gathered at his bedside were to remember the wisdom of the wild things, to trust the baptism of the elements, and always to honor the healing power of the waters. Many said that he was the greatest of the *Celli Dé*, and that his life was an example of the way that men and women should follow who would learn the wisdom of the great creation.

❖ ❖ ❖

Kentigern's life contains many riddles that, if we look at them open-eyed, we can begin to understand. From the beginning his life is affected by the four primary elements of earth, air, fire, and water. His mother suffers two punishments, those of air (by falling down from the high place) and water (by her journey at the mercy of the sea). Kentigern himself, like so many of his fellows, is constantly in touch with the natural world in this way. He brings to life the dead bird beloved of his master by breathing the breath of life into it; he shows his command of the element of fire by lighting the candles in the church from the branch that bursts into flame at his wish; he heals the mad Lailocen through water; he is linked to the earth through animals—as when he is led to the site of his future monastic settlement by a white boar, an animal ever held sacred by the Celts, and when he recovers the lost ring from the body of a fish (to this day Kentigern's insignia are a salmon and a ring). In addition, he suffers a near death from cold (another elemental challenge) before being released by his novice Asaph, who is able to carry hot coals to warm him without suffering harm.

It may well be that behind the story of Kentigern lies a far older tradition concerning an ancient solar hero. His mysterious birth (watched over by shepherds) is reminiscent of that of more than one wonder-child, including Christ, the Roman Mithras, and the Middle Eastern Attis. Each episode in his life has to do with an element in one way or another, and these are clearly Kentigern's link with the infinite life of the spirit. His soul's journey is through contact with the presence of the divine in the elemental world, and through this he is able to bring healing as well as wisdom to those in need.

Among the Celts the elements were always perceived as doorways into an infinite universe. Fire was the fire of inspiration, and brought the other elements in its train. The ancient and semimythical Irish poet Amairgin expressed it thus:

> I am a wind on the sea,
> I am a wave on the ocean,
> I am the roar in the sea . . .
> I am a tear in the sun,
> I am a salmon in a pool . . .
> I am a god who fashions fire in the mind . . .
> —Trans. J. M.

Water was the way between the worlds, whether by way of the voyage that led out of this world, out of ordinary reality, into another place, or through imbibing the stuff of wonder and mystery from one of the many sacred cauldrons or wells that appear so often in the ancient Celtic tradition. Again and again we find references in Celtic literature to the power of water to transform the individual, to act as a conductor for the most profound mysteries.

An ancient Gaelic prayer says: "May God give you to drink from the Cauldron that never runs dry," a reference to the many wondrous vessels of plenty and inspiration that are found scattered throughout Celtic tradition. Thus the sixth-century Welsh shaman-poet Taliesin imbibes universal wisdom from a cauldron in which has been brewed a distillation of all knowledge. Once he has drunk this he goes through a series of transformations that take him through each of the elements: he turns into an animal, a fish, a bird, and a grain of parched wheat. Afterward he has the knowledge of each element, which instructs him in a better understanding of all created life.

We too can learn by observing and honoring the elements around us. Every day we breathe air, warm ourselves by fire, bathe in water, and walk upon the earth; yet we seldom if ever notice or acknowledge the divine presence within each of them. Breath itself has always been seen as the purveyor of life, and for this reason perhaps the Celts perceived the winds as bringing either good or bad fortune in their wake. According to early tradition, there were twelve such winds, each one blowing from a different direction and given a different color, name, and attribute. Solanus, the wind that blew in January, brought plague and disease; Africus, which blew from the southeast, was especially good for the propagation of fruit; Saronicus, from the south, was deemed to bring a good harvest; and so on.

In our own lives we seldom orient ourselves to the directions or recognize the elemental quality they each carry. The oldest known European traditions of the West designate the cardinal points of the compass with an element. North is equated with earth, south with fire, east with air, and west with water. These qualities themselves bear other references to less abstract things: North has to do with strength and the things that sustain us, such as hearth and home, family and friends. South brings us closer to the fires of inspiration and the energies of life itself, through creativity and the imagination. West has to do with the emotions, with love, hate, sorrow, and joy, and the freedom of tears. East brings us the gifts of the spirit and connects us to all living beings.

By learning to resonate with the directions in our own lives, we can learn from them just as Kentigern did. Through being aware of the power of the directions, and by acknowledging them every day, we can enter into a greater harmony with the universe around us— the final goal of all spiritual seekers. We may never bring back birds from the dead, or learn to foretell the future, but we can come to terms with some of the tests that life daily offers us.

❊ ❊ ❊

Meditation Points

- Consider how you relate to the four primary directions and the elements they represent. What is your relationship to the earth beneath your feet? To the sky above you? To the air you breathe? To the water you drink or in which you cleanse yourself? How do you respond to the element of fire?

- Over four days try to be as fully aware of each element as possible, giving your attention to one on each successive day. Look within to see how they affect you, and when you have done so, honor them in whatever way seems best to you.

❈ ❈ ❈

Calendar of the Birds

Birds of the world, bright without shame,
it is to welcome the sun again;
at the nones of January, whatever the hour,
a host consorts in the sheltering wood.

On the eighth of the calends of eminent April
Flights of swallows make congregation;
a strand of exile their concealment
from the eighth of the calends of October.

On the feast of Ruadan, runs the saying,
all their fetters are unlocked;
on the seventeenth of the calends of May,
unceasing cuckoos throng the wood.

In Tallaght the birds relent their
sung music on the July calends
for Mael Ruan, whom the Badbh took not:
the living pray on that woeful day.

On Ciaran's feast, son of the smith,
the barnacle goose flies over cold seas;
on Cyprian's feast, a great contention,
the brown stag bells from the red plains.

Three score thousand years of whiteness
is the term of the world, without doubt;
billows will burst across every airt*
at the end of night, at the cry of birds.

Renewing is the melodious music
of birds to the King of the bright clouds,
their praise to the King of stars:
listen to the feathered choir afar!

—*Fourteenth-century Irish; trans. Caitlín Matthews*

* *direction*

Sources and Further Reading

Lives of the Celtic Saints

Adamnan. *The Life of St Columba*. Edited by William Reeves. Llanerch, Dyfed: Llanerch Enterprises, 1998.

Ailred. "The Life of St Ninian." In *Two Celtic Saints*. Llanerch, Dyfed: Llanerch Enterprises, 1989.

Curtayne, Alice. *St Brigit of Ireland*. New York: Sheed & Ward, 1954.

Gould, S. Baring, and John Fisher. *Lives of the British Saints*. Edited by Derek Bryce. Llanerch, Dyfed: Llanerch Enterprises, 1990.

Joceline. "The Life of St Kentigern." In *Two Celtic Saints*. Llanerch, Dyfed: Llanerch Enterprises, 1989.

O Domhnaill, Maghnas. *Betha Colaim Chille*. Edited by A. O'Kelleher and G. Schoepperle. Dublin: Institute for Advanced Studies, reprinted 1994.

O'Mera, John. *The Voyage of St Brendan*. Dublin: Dolmen Press, 1978, 1997.

Plummer, Charles, ed. and trans. *Lives of Irish Saints*. 2 vols. Oxford: Oxford Univ. Press, 1922.

Stokes, Whitley. *Lives of the Saints from the Book of Lismore*. Felinfach: Llanerch Enterprises, 1995.

———. *The Martyrology of Oengus the Culdee*. Dublin: Institute for Advanced Studies, 1984.

Further Reading

Bamford, Christopher. *The Voice of the Eagle: Homily on the Prologue to the Gospel of St John by John Scotus Eriugena.* Hudson, NY: Lindisfarne Press, 1990.

Bamford, Christopher, and William Parker Marsh. *Celtic Christianity: Ecology and Holiness.* West Stockbridge, MA: Lindisfarne Press, 1986.

Borlase, William C. *The Age of the Saints: A Monograph of Early Christianity in Cornwall.* Felinfach: Llanerch Enterprises, 1995.

Caine, Mary. *Celtic Saints and the Glastonbury Zodiac.* Chieveley, Berks: Capall Bann Publishing, 1998.

Carey, John. *King of Mysteries: Irish Religion Writings, 600–1200.* Dublin: Four Courts Press, 1998.

Carmichael, Alexander. *Carmina Gadelica: Hymns and Incantations.* Edinburgh: Floris Books, 1992.

Chadwick, Nora K. *The Age of the Saints in the Celtic Church.* Oxford: Oxford Univ. Press, 1961.

Clancy, Thomas Owen, and Gilbert Markus. *Iona: The Earliest Poetry of a Celtic Monastery.* Edinburgh: Edinburgh Univ. Press, 1995.

Darcy, Mary Ryan. *The Saints of Ireland.* Cork and Dublin: Mercier Press, 1974.

Davies, Oliver. *Celtic Christianity in Early Medieval Wales.* Cardiff: Univ. of Wales Press, 1996.

Davies, Wendy. "The Myth of the Celtic Church." In *The Early Church in the West.* Edited by Nancy Edwards and Alan Lane. Oxbow Monographs No. 16. Oxford: Oxbow Books, 1992.

De Waal, Esther. *The Celtic Vision.* London: Darton, Longman & Todd, 1988.

Farmer, David Hugh. *The Oxford Dictionary of Saints*. Oxford: Clarendon Press, 1978.

Gregory, Lady Augusta. *Book of Saints and Wonders*. London: Colin Smyth, 1971.

Henken, Elissa R. *Traditions of the Welsh Saints*. Cambridge, England: D. S. Brewer, 1987.

Hyde, Douglas. *Legends of Saints and Sinners*. London: T. Fisher Unwin, 1896.

Irvine, John. *A Treasury of Irish Saints*. Dublin: Dolmen Press, 1964.

Lehane, Brendan. *The Quest of Three Abbots*. Hudson, NY: Lindisfarne Press, 1994.

Low, Mary. *Celtic Christianity and Nature*. Edinburgh: Edinburgh Univ. Press, 1974.

Lynch, Patricia. *Knights of God*. London: Bodley Head, 1967.

Maclean, Alistair. *Hebridean Altars*. Edinburgh: Moray Press, 1923.

McNeill, John. *The Celtic Churches*. Chicago: Univ. of Chicago Press, 1974.

Marsden, John. *Sea-Road of the Saints: Celtic Holy Men in the Hebrides*. Edinburgh: Floris Books, 1995.

Marshall, Peter. *Celtic Gold: A Voyage Around Ireland*. London: Sinclair-Stevenson, 1997.

Matthews, Caitlín. *The Celtic Book of the Dead*. New York: St. Martin's Press, 1992.

———. *A Celtic Devotional*. New Alresford, Hants: Godsfield Press, 1997.

———. *Singing the Soul Back Home*. Shaftsbury, Dorset: Element Books, 1996.

Matthews, John. *The Celtic Shaman*. Shaftsbury, Dorset: Element Books, 1995.

Matthews, John, and Caitlín Matthews. *The Encyclopedia of Celtic Wisdom*. Shaftsbury, Dorset: Element Books, 1994.

Mayo, Margaret. *Saints, Birds, and Beasts*. London: Kaye & Ward, 1980.

Melia, Daniel. "The Irish Saint as Shaman." *Pacific Coast Philology* 18 (1983): 37–42.

Meyer, Kuno. *Ancient Irish Poetry*. London: Constable, 1913.

Nagy, Joseph Falaky. *Conversing with Angels and Ancients*. Dublin: Four Courts Press, 1997.

O'Donoghue, John. *Anam Cara: Spiritual Wisdom from the Celtic World*. New York and London: Bantam Press, 1997.

O Fiaich, Tomas. *Columbanus in His Own Words*. Dublin: Veritas, 1974.

Pennick, Nigel. *The Celtic Saints*. London: Thorsons/Godsfield Press, 1997.

Ryan, John. *Irish Monasticism*. Ithaca, NY: Cornell Univ. Press, 1972.

Sellner, Edward C. *Wisdom of the Celtic Saints*. Notre Dame, IN: Ave Maria Press, 1993.

Thomas, Patrick. *Candle in the Darkness: Celtic Spirituality from Wales*. Llandysul, Dyfed: Gomer Press, 1994.

Van der Weyer, Robert. *Celtic Fire*. New York and London: Doubleday, 1991.